For the Dying Calves

THE GERMAN LIST

DURS GRÜNBEIN

For the Dying Calves

BEYOND LITERATURE

Oxford Lectures

Translated by Karen Leeder

LONDON NEW YORK CALCUTTA

This publication has been supported by a grant from
the Goethe-Institut India

Seagull Books, 2021

Originally published in German as *Jenseits der Literatur - Oxford Lectures*
by Durs Grünbein

© Suhrkamp Verlag, Berlin, 2020

First published in English translation by Seagull Books, 2021

English translation © Karen Leeder, 2021

'Highway' by Adam Zagajewski on page 64 excerpted from *Asymmetry: Poems*
(Clare Cavanagh trans.) (New York: Farrar, Straus and Giroux, 2018).
Reproduced with kind permission from Farrar, Straus and Giroux.

Durs Grünbein's poem 'Accept It!' on pages 113–14 has been translated
from the original German by Karen Leeder

ISBN 978 0 8574 2 954 4

British Library Cataloguing-in-Publication Data
A catalogue record for this book is available from the British Library

Typeset by Seagull Books, Calcutta, India
Printed and bound by in the USA by Integrated Books International

CONTENTS

I

THE VIOLET POSTAGE STAMP

When I recall my childhood stamp collection, the first thing that comes to mind is a detail that could be the stuff of dreams—so vividly and insistently does it dance before my eyes—a small, square butterfly, the colour of vitriol. There was an album, hoarded like a forbidden treasure, where I kept stamps from the Third Reich, including a series in various hues featuring the head of the man whose name could only be whispered behind closed doors. What did I, as a child, know then about the cursed Austrian, the man from Braunau am Inn who wrote himself into the course of Germany history, and changed it, like no other?

The stamps in this most dangerous of all my albums had all been put in the wrong way up. The seducer of the German people with his dark brooding glare and his neatly parted hair was upside down. Had I done that and why? I no longer recall: was it was a precaution in case anyone discovered my album by accident; or an act of exorcism, decapitating this villain, this arch-Dervish of all things German?

All I know is that the sight of stamps inevitably leads me back to a paradise of memory, a horticultural spectacle within the tiniest compass. A whole world preserved in miniature pictures behind the see-through retaining strips of the collector's album. Postage stamps are often the first *Orbis Pictus* in the life of a child. There in miniature, they spread out before you a book of the visible world, in the manner of the illustrated primer of the Czech theologian Johann Amos Comenius. The rows of stamps reminded me of flowerbeds, carefully ordered and tended and yet whirling together in a wild confusion with their bright and endlessly varied motifs. A group of traditional costumes next to the drilling rig; a squirrel on a tree trunk next to the Olympic-champion ski-jumper—gems of philately from all over the world, with the bright colours of circus posters. There were the ones from the Maldives with their strange triangular shape, and right next to them the oversized Brazilian ones with the magnificent butterfly illustrations.

The survivors from the Nazi years seemed strangely austere and monotonous in comparison. They were uninspired in a rather oppressive way, modest in the range of images—there were only eagles and castles, brutal-looking men in steel helmets, equestrians and naked athletes, and later images of infantry in action with a variety of weapons. Every so often though, one glimpsed the dictator in profile, cast as a visionary statesman. I don't know what had got into us, but back then this most repulsive figure of the age appeared to us like a character from some dark fairy tale. He was the demon we hoped to ward off with a ban on images, a general taboo.

I had given up stamp-collecting at some point; the albums vanished into the attic like so much else. Years later, as I was leafing through them, a battlefield postcard fluttered into my hands with a violet postage stamp. It was its provocative hue, the purple of wolf's-bane, that set my thoughts racing in strange directions. The same print of the *Führer*'s head existed in pea green, chestnut brown, blood

2

red, it even popped up in the harmless orange colour of southern fruit. Letters and postcards bearing the threatening likeness had been sent out into all corners of the world. Loaded onto express trains, they criss-crossed the *awakening* Fatherland and were dispatched by airmail as far as America, China and Australia. When I think back now to all those uniform little stamps, the mass character of National Socialism becomes immediately apparent. I ask myself how many million people must have licked Hitler at that time, willingly or unwillingly, but licked him nonetheless. This vision of multi-tongued slavishness, silver-tongued duplicity, sticky servility has something repulsive about it.

If it wasn't the sponge on the post-office counter, then a human tongue must have moistened the reverse. I imagine all the times that happened, all those unnoticed, intimate moments, the occasions involved and the different sites within the new European theatre of war. The bright July day at a table in a Munich beer garden, or late summer in Vienna sitting beneath the vine tendrils, drinking the early wine and sending greetings to loved ones at home. A postcard to an aunt, sealed with a thump of the fist on the obstinate stamp when the soldier's mate had disappeared to the toilet. Or sticking one onto the *billet doux* intended for the beloved, in high spirits, months before the order to leave for the front. A winter evening in the guardroom of a barracks in Occupied Poland, forces mail after leave in Warsaw, walking alongside the fences of the newly erected ghetto; one soldier writing to his mother: 'It's still crawling with Jews here.' Or sent from a barracks in Occupied Lublin on the anniversary of 'Two Years of General Government' in Poland. From a Berlin dive after a sleepless night, hours before boarding the troop trains to Russia.

3

Each time it was the same unconscious act, something an ape might do—like picking over a coat for lice, licking a stick covered with ants—a conditioned reflex; one of many necessities in our modern life. People who caught themselves doing it were likely ashamed for a split second, then came a passing anxiety about catching something, but the next moment it was forgotten, and they had already moistened the next stamp.

The six-pfennig violet postage stamp with the image of Hitler and the words *Deutsches Reich*—like a poisonous plant, some kind of bog flower—was stuck on all the postcards of the time. I remember how I gazed at it the first time I saw it—knowing full well that I was doing something forbidden. That's the moment I was swallowed down into that little square of colour—like curious Alice falling down the rabbit hole—and ended up lost between times and signs. It is how a hiker must feel when he comes across a rare edelweiss flower in the mountains.

Later, when this stamp occasionally crossed my path, something of that sense of the monstrous still seemed to reverberate down the years, the shameful experience of having crashed through unstable ground. Without warning I had been drawn down through this tiny membrane and into the most grisly chapter of German history. Much later in Vladimir Nabokov's memoirs, *Speak, Memory*, I came across a passage that brought my stamp collection (long since vanished) vividly back to mind. The narrator is telling a story about his exile in 1930s Berlin and explains how he had often sought out public parks to take his child little Dimitri to play.

Our child must have been almost three on that breezy day in Berlin (where of course no one could escape the

4

familiarity with the ubiquitous picture of the *Führer*) when we stood, he and I, before a bed of pale pansies, each of their upturned faces showing a dark moustache-like smudge, and had great fun, at my rather silly prompting, commenting on their resemblance to a crowd of bobbing little Hitlers.

It was the similarity with something that seemed intrinsically natural, a pattern of flowers, the impression simply of shape and colour, that had left me in such turmoil when I looked at my stamp collection. The violet postage stamp, long since slipped from my memory, was suddenly there again, growing bigger and smaller and oscillating between a brutal proximity and a dizzying distance. In this scrap of paper with its perforated edges, something had become intrinsically tangible: the equation that linked the individual and the masses. The violet stamp with the profile of the *Führer* was an abyss that could open at any time. Here, on one side, the individual, now one in a series of images, the man from the men's hostel in Vienna, the inferior figure—*A nameless man, one among millions of others*—as he described himself in his account of his struggle, *Mein Kampf*. And there, on the other side, a people largely made up of the destitute and disillusioned, a people that raised this sorry article from among their midst to the highest rank—while they themselves constituted the nameless millions of the mass. The postage stamp stood for the random individual, the one who turned himself into the medium of the many, who for their part, marked the zenith of his meteoric rise by immortalizing him as the model of charismatic leadership on millions of stamps that now whizzed back and forth across the German Reich. As for them, all they could do was stare helplessly as they affixed the stamp, just as I had stared at him, this most unfamiliar of all familiars, with his precisely parted hair and striking nose, gazing fixedly to the right into a future that, thank God, never came to pass. Now they were all subject to his compulsive momentum, caught up in a mass movement. The postal service was the only thing that allowed them to keep in contact with one another, now that everything had been turned upside down in this German nation turbulent to its core.

Even the specially designed postmarks stamped over the postage stamps or just beside them began to gain their own meaning; not immediately, but gradually, as the sense of historical events took hold. The constant stream of daily orders and announcements, the grand campaigns with which the sender of the letter became associated whether he wished or not: *Nuremburg Party Convention! Saarland Becomes German! Collection for Strength through Joy! International Hunting Exhibition! Be on Your Guard with Fire in Wood and Field! Horse Race—Das braune Band! Breslau National Gymnastic and Sport Festival! Munich: Capital City of the Movement! State Visit: Hitler and Mussolini! Sudeten-Land German! The Führer in Vienna! Leipzig: Reich Trade Fair!* And when Czechoslovakia was annexed despite all the assurances: *We Thank Our Führer! Panzer Division Leibstandarte SS—Adolf Hitler! Exhibition: The*

Soviet Paradise! Rye Bread: Better and Healthier! Avoid Radio Interference! Send Your Christmas Parcels Promptly! Then, when the War had begun, and Germany was advancing on all fronts yet simultaneously found itself isolated from the rest of the world: *Winter Relief! Necessary Air-Raid Protection! War Relief for the Red Cross! Training Month of the SA! Book Parcels from the NSDP for Our Army!* Then suddenly Europe became the new slogan: *Europe's United Front against Bolshevism! Founding Conference of the European Youth Movement!* And after the turning point of Stalingrad: *They Died for Greater Germany! Dedicated to Their Sacrifice! Germany Will Be Victorious!* But then when all hopes were dashed: *Your Attitude Is Decisive! Commission for Ceasefire!*

Twelve years of collective brain washing, rallying calls, an uninterrupted barrage of propaganda. And amid all this, as if everything was entirely normal, the quaint refrain of the philatelists, each and every year right up to the end of the war: *Day of Stamps! German Philatelists Day!* There was local advertising too; tourist post-marks: *Landshut Wedding! Schaefer's Lilliputian Fairy Tale Town! Stralau Fisherman's Festival Berlin Treptow 1936! Rosenheim Autumn Festival! Berlin Automobile Show! Garmisch-Partenkirchen International Week of Winter Sports 1941! German Regional Bowling Tournament Frankfurt am Main!* Then there were the nationwide announcements: *Harvest Festival! Combat the Potato Beetle!* And, every year, one for the chronicler rather than the collector: *The Führer's Birthday!*

Considered as examples of advertising, these were pioneering advances of a postal aesthetic that is still in use today. In the early years, while stocks lasted, the great head of Hindenburg, the venerable Prussian dome of the Reichsmarschall, was still in circulation. Perhaps a sign of secret opposition or lost hope on the part of the senders, many of whom knew all too well what had been, and were gradually beginning to fear what was coming? Signals from those who thought differently? Who knows? The thick-skulled Hindenburg, styled as Victor of the Battle of Tannenburg, still crops up regularly on some of the very last letters from the battlefields. What were the members of the armed forces thinking when they handed over letters and cards at the field post station, while at home their mothers and fathers were waiting for word as the cities sank in rubble and ash around them?

But by that point it was far too late. There was nothing to be done about the other head, no quarter against the moustachioed postage-stamp king with the dark look of a redeemer. His portrait was now ubiquitous, found in every corner of the Reich. His likeness hung in every office, every classroom, every meeting room of the Army, Party, or Reich Labour Services, and it was impossible to imagine it any other way. Only the sensitive experience this kind of ubiquity as a personal catastrophe: their own facial features devalued like those of all others, until they became part of a community of people who had already gone so far there was no turning back. Their individual fates melted into a single catastrophic chain of disasters.

But there were exceptions too, of course there were: lives that followed unusual paths and played out in different ways, completely outside the norm. Like that of Edmund Kalb, a painter from Dornbirn in the Vorarlberg; an Austrian who could never accept the annexation, the absolute antithesis of Hitler. Kalb embodied the 'artist as outsider'; he was never allowed to live as an artist, so

became a lifelong outsider. A painter just like the one born in Braunau am Inn who, when he could not become an artist, started a movement of his own and made all Germany into a *Gesamtkunstwerk* with the total destruction of the nation as the dark culmination. Edmund Kalb, in contrast, born eleven years after Hitler, left behind an oeuvre consisting of more than a thousand self-portraits. A body of work born as a kind of self-defence: an attempt to counter the general loss of face under the diktat of this one face, this ' . . . jelly-like, slag-grey, sallow moonface', as another outsider, the doctor Friedrich Reck-Malleczewen, called it in his *Tagebuch eines Verzweifelten* (Diary of a Man in Despair). Kalb is the perfect example of the fate of a poor wretch in a country that allows itself to be led by a band of criminals. Economic necessity forces him to break off his studies at the Academy of Fine Arts in Munich and to return to his parents' home.

9

No one in his rural surroundings understands him; for the rest of his life he remains an oddity in their eyes. After the Annexation of Austria, his situation becomes more acute. In January 1942 he is called up into the army and finds himself in pretty much constant conflict with his superiors. He spends nearly the whole of the war in detention, moved on from one military prison to another. His psychiatric file notes that he could not bear being shouted at; that in the end he began to feel at home in his cell and look for opportunities to be locked up as often as possible, so that he could begin to enjoy the long-sought-after peace that had eluded him on the outside and spend his time considering mathematical conundrums. During this time, he continued a lively correspondence with his father and other relatives; and on all the many letters he sent, the stamps with the portrait of Hitler on were always cut in half, as an occult act, a kind of black magic. Now and then he goes as far as mocking the cult of the *Führer* by completely covering the back of the envelopes with one-pfennig stamps, all bearing Hitler's head and sometimes arranged in patterns. The despairing actions of a humourist: evidently one could only exorcise this man by multiplying his image to the point of absurdity. But he could not, alas, be destroyed in this way; like a devil he survived precisely in the image. To this very day he possesses the gift of all truly undead: he always returns. Hundreds of times a year he celebrates his resurrection across all the TV channels, in programmes like *Hitler's Paladins, Hitler's Women, Hitler's Blitzkrieg* or *Obersalzburg: Hitler's Mountain Hideaway* (in colour).

Edmund Kalb on the other hand—even his surname Kalb (calf) seems to have marked out his fate—was a monomaniacal artist, unrecognized and misunderstood during his lifetime, above

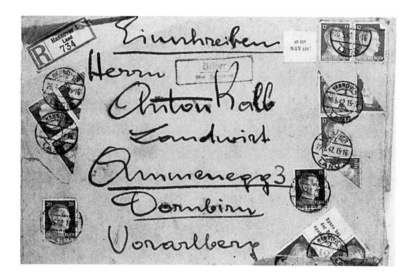

all by his own family, who denied him and were ashamed of what the doctors treating him called a 'querulous psychopath' in their midst. Kalb was the undaunted one for whom there was truly no hope. The list of his crimes was long: obstructing officers in the performance of their duty; insubordination; insulting an official; holding an expert psychiatric assessment in contempt. And it is no chance that his martyrdom continued long after the war had finished. He got into bother straightaway. And each time he was arrested he made sure he created a public spectacle. Witnesses report that one of the many times he was being escorted from the scene, of necessity by car on account of the disturbance he had caused, he kept reaching out of the windows to show people the bar chain on his hands. Once when being interrogated, at a point when it could still have cost him his life, he placed on record the simple thought that, if Hitler could do anything, then he should solve the squaring of the circle or the square root of two—only then would he believe this man so mighty. It is a wonder that Kalb was not simply shot on the spot. He was forever putting himself in situations that sealed the fate of other dissidents in the Third Reich.

By February 1945 he found himself imprisoned close to Dessau. With the approach of the English forces, he was assigned a dedicated guard and moved on from prison to prison in splendid isolation. In this way he ended up reaching Prague in the final days of the war. Imagine: a German soldier, a deserter to the depths of his soul, deserting not merely from this senseless war but also from Hitler's Reich and from the whole German Volk obedient to their *Führer*, simply manages to say no, like Bartelby the Scrivener in Herman Melville's story, and survives because he cannot be grasped in his defiance—a defiance that simply rejects the collective events going on around him. And he knows how to tell his story and keep a record of the injustices done to him. When he is finally released from his last prison he goes back to his roots. A vegetarian (like Franz Kafka and his existential opposite Adolf Hitler), he makes ends meet by growing vegetables and grain in a small holding that allows him to be self-sufficient. He experiments with grafting trees and even tries bud grafts of several fruit trees. Many years after his death his family can still, as they say, harvest barrels full of pears and plums from trees he had grafted. Finally, he begins to cultivate rice in Dornbirn encouraged by specialist literature from Russia describing experiments to do the same in Siberia. And all this he records in diary entries, like the stations of his life, as small as a postage stamp. He is conscious—just like Pascal and Ludwig Wittgenstein before him—that everything he does follows its own inner necessity and must be done.

One day in the very depths of confusion he holds onto a single idea: that the multitude of thoughts that accompany someone as

they observe the world around them can never be expressed in words—rather, if at all, and then only with a little bit of luck—by means of drawings. His diaries often return to this imbalance between words and images. Once he writes with a wistfulness born of the realization that it is impossible ever to bring the richness of one's inner life onto the page: 'I only regret that there is no means of transmitting and recording an emotional experience per se, as it is experienced *in statu nascendi*. If there were, people would have more consideration for one another and more willingness to understand one another.'

Hitler's face, notes the furious Reck-Malleczewen in his diary, having seen Hitler close up in Munich, 'is a wretched excremental visage, every inch a middle-class antichrist'. What would you do, I asked myself, if an all-powerful face like that turned up in your time and cast a shadow over your life?

But that is exactly how it was. In my childhood and during my time at school there were ubiquitous portraits of Lenin on posters and in textbooks. Joseph Brodsky, another one to have been plagued by omnipresent images of leaders, wrote: 'In a certain way this face pursues every Russian and offers a model for the standard appearance because it is totally devoid of any trace of character.' There were colour photos of General Secretary Erich Honecker in every office up and down the country, and in the first years of my existence there were even stamps with the profile of the previous president, Water Ulbricht. Green stamps they were, red and blue ones too. The Communist Party leader from Saxony looked like everyone's good uncle with his trim little pointed beard. One could even think of him as the Santa Claus of socialism. I come across these stamps on the letters I sent home from holiday camps. Today they seem to me like historical nothings. Who was Walter Ulbricht, after all, to earn a postage stamp of his own? Philatelists will be able to gauge a particular historical moment by them. But they will never inspire fear and horror like the sight of the violet Hitler. Nothing is comparable to the megalomaniacal grandeur that this one person exuded, even in effigy, and even beyond his death.

I still recall how I came across him for the first time, while staying with my grandparents in Gotha when I was a child of about ten or eleven. Exploring the ancient house in Querstrasse, I suddenly encountered something obscene. It was a find no one had prepared me for, something so shrouded in silence that I felt like a thief intruding on a family secret. It was that moment of trespass when an inner voice tells you: you must never tell a soul. I found it hidden underneath bundles of papers, in a dresser in the airing loft. The entrance to this space was barred with wooden railings and lay half a staircase lower than my grandparents' flat. This strange unplace, on a kind of mezzanine landing, was one of the many curiosities of this labyrinthine baroque house that confused a child's sense of orientation—with its corridors on every floor full of nooks and crannies, and a cellar under the baker's shop on the ground floor that seemed to gape like a pit shaft with its precipitously sloping passageways.

Now, poking around in this old house was exciting enough at that age; but suddenly I had stumbled on a trap. I had been rummaging around and came upon the dresser with its tempting drawers. And there was the book with its dark-blue binding, swollen with damp. The corners were tatty, gnawed by rats or mice, the cover hung loose. What I found was a yellowed, raddled copy of *Mein Kampf*.

It was, as was explained to me many years later by an expert, the so-called wedding edition of the German People's Book. My grandparents had married in the mid-1930s in the little town of Langensalza in Thuringia. The person officiating at the ceremony had, as was customary in the Third Reich, solemnly handed a copy of the New Gospel of the age, inscribed 'to the newlyweds with best wishes for a happy and blessed union'. Whether out of false pride or sentiment, in any case, the dangerous tome had been stashed away here beyond the end of the war with the inevitable danger of a raid by Russian soldiers. The inflammatory work had been hidden away instead of quietly disposed of, as was fitting after the downfall of the Reich. No doubt it was my grandfather who had kept the book, out of a kind of piety towards the *Führer*, his highest commander, to whom he had sworn an oath of loyalty as a policeman, a lifetime official of the town of Gotha, and to whom he felt himself beholden even after Hitler's death. He had been appointed in his name and as it stated in the articles of his appointment he could count on '*the special protection of the Führer*'.

I don't know how long it was that I gazed down at the visage of the highest marriage witness in the land. I had opened the book and there he was: Hitler—a photograph taken front on, the only illustration, set before the text as a brutal introduction. He was wearing the brown shirt of the SA and the peaked cap, a leather strap stretched diagonally across his uniformed breast. His face was polished with the lustre of a pair of boots, the face of a wax figure tensed and flickering with an inner mania. This was clearly a man prepared to do anything, this was how he had presented himself to the camera. Heinrich Hoffmann, his court photographer—founder of the Munich studio Photohaus Hoffmann where the young Eva Braun did her apprenticeship, and where, legend has it, Hitler first encountered her—Hoffmann had orchestrated the image of his master like this. He was the advertising guru of the brown movement.

Adolf Hitler looked deep into the viewer's eyes like someone about to cast a spell on millions. He had put on his famous loyal sheepdog expression, the sparkling animal gaze of the hypnotist demanding unconditional loyalty. I never came closer to this man of horror than in that moment. As a child I had without knowing walked straight into a trap. The theatricality of it all I only grasped many years later, the actor's con trick, his method of digging deep into the hearts of the autograph hunters with his studied poses. So too, that everything in the Third Reich was a matter of conscious orchestration, including the falsified facts, because here for the first time a regime was at work that manipulated every relationship with

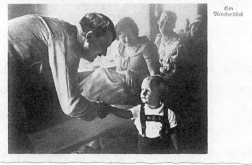

Ein
Kinderblick

an eye to the media—including and above all the relationship between individual and the masses, between propaganda and reality, great and small.

What did I know then of the photo technicians and their tricks of the trade; of Hitler's camera man and his test shots of the soon-to-be politician in striking orator's poses in his studio? Or that Hoffmann alone came to enjoy the privilege of photographing the dictator close up, and that every official image of the leader had to go through him and later the Reich press desk for the purpose of censorship before it was permitted to enter mass circulation? For me a photo was a photo, I was a naive child. If someone had attempted to explain photomontage to me, the technique would have seemed like a bizarre ruse from the world of grownups.

Of course, I could tell nobody about my discovery. A line had been crossed and I knew it instinctively. Driven by curiosity and through sheer dumb luck, I had ventured into the junk room of German history. I had become complicit in a family secret so dirty that it could not be discussed with a living soul. Asking my grandparents about it was impossible, I would have had to admit that I had been rummaging round in their private lives. I felt bad, bad three times over—as a rat rooting around in their private things, a chicken, now not wanting to say anything, and the wayward grandson that had trespassed into forbidden territory. It was all my fault. Hitler the magician from the land of the Nazis had caught me out when I took my eye off the ball for a second. From that moment on this person had power over me and over my little life that only yesterday had been untouched by history. A school child on holiday with his grandparents during the summer holidays, yes, I too had fallen under his spell.

Over the years I like everyone else have learnt to come to terms with the fatal legacy. I have never made peace with it though—how could I? After history lessons at school, after all the anti-Fascist indoctrination, after repeated visits to concentrations camps (Buchenwald, Ravensbrück, Sachsenhausen), after every visit to an exhibition about National Socialism, I still found myself seized by a profound dread. Once our class had been visiting Ettersberg; we had been shown the lampshades made of human skin in Buchenwald and the room with the measuring device designed to disguise a fatal shot to the neck of the prisoners. The father of one of my schoolmates, the son of a Hellerau surgeon, had been interned there. During the preparation classes for the *Jugendweihe*, or coming-of-age ceremony, he had come into to school to describe the various methods of torture. A small, bent man whom I sometimes saw at the bakery down on the market square, a distinguished anti-Fascist.

But also, in those quiet moments of contemplation, rooting around at flea markets, weighing up my antiquarian finds—postcards, books, photographs—the agitation could return out of the blue. Over the years it grew to become a powerful depression triggered by memory.

I remember it struck me once when I was in the Berlin Postal Museum in Leipziger Strasse and found myself suddenly standing in front of a blood-red postbox. The colour of the Reich-Post in the Greater German Reich was red—a pure sensation of colour. Just an object; and what could be more harmless or innocent than a postbox? There is little in day-to-day life as heartening as the yellow postboxes on the street corners of the town. A postbox looms into view and the child's heart fizzes with joy. I remember it with my daughters, each of them almost as soon as they could stretch on tiptoes, would beg to be allowed to slide the letter or postcard into the slot themselves.

This was the focal point of our longings. Here one could pause in a moment of regulated, well-functioning love of the distant goal. I have watched as people have hesitated before posting their letter, smiling and lost in thought for a moment. And now suddenly this red postbox in front of me. Incomprehensible. Red letterboxes like this had once stood all over Germany. Red telephone boxes lined the streets of the inner cities from Breisgau to Gdansk just a year after the Nazi accession to power. From one end of the country to the other, the bright red postal vans delivered letters and parcels, oversized lorries with massive horsepower that made a bigger impression than the fire engines today, whereas the historical fire trucks that meandered through the bombed rubble of the cities after the sirens had sounded were painted deep green like the German forest or black as night.

What did all these signals mean? Did the colours change with the political regime? The black uniforms of the SS Death's head units, the brown uniforms of their precursors, the goon squads of the SA, or the once green now standard blue (European blue) service dress of the police force in the Federal Republic. Colour, it seems, is always the last prevailing level of abstraction in every social organization. Why is the fire service red today and the postal service a uniform yellow, I ask myself, as I wander through Berlin at night and tug the dog round the postboxes after me? 'A man lost in time / near KaDeWe' sings David Bowie in one of his melancholy songs before he disappeared with the question 'Where are we now?'

Colour and memory: in fashion, in politics, even in poetry, colour seems to play a uniquely important role. What was the meaning of the different colours of different political movements? What was their function? Blue for Europe; yellow for the Liberals; while neo-Nazis still prefer black: black bomber jackets and back boots—death-chic.

Why the standardized bodily colour? Did it exist in the animal kingdom? And if so, what was the function there? Were there evolutionary reasons for the coloration of animals of the same species?

Rapid recognition, mating signals, deterrence of natural enemies, protection from infection, reproductive advantages, or advantage in foraging for food?

'In red', it said in the book I found in my grandparents' attic, 'we see the social thinking of the movement, in white the rationalist, in the swastika the mission of the struggle, the victory of Aryanism and along with it, the victory of thought, of work, that itself has always been anti-Semitic and always will be.'

There was also the issue of disguise; camouflage was a military matter. But why red, the colour of blood, long since synonymous with the call to reach for a better world in the form of Communism, that mobilized so many hearts in the name of equality, the just distribution of goods? The Red Front, the red star of the Soviet Union and even the pale red of the Social Democrats. Whereas brown was the common denominator in colour terms for a movement in which the retrograde forged the way: resentment, racism, the principle of violence, and a chauvinist sense of solidarity. 'It is difficult to comprehend', writes Hitler's first biographer, Konrad Heiden, 'why precisely this pale yellowish-brown, probably the ugliest in the whole colour palette, was chosen to become the symbol of the movement'. The obvious thought is that a certain unhealthy feeling played its part in choosing this garish colour of dirt. References to elements of the erotic in the comradeship of the male SA regiments and to Freud's anal stage of psychosexual development are one thing. Quite another is the notion of political regression in and of itself that is expressed in this greasy brown. Cack brown, the colour characteristic of a politics of rumination and digestion, after a phrase from Karl Marx and Friedrich Engels—for *the same old crap.*

I remember first coming across the quotation during a lecture on political economics at the Humboldt University in Berlin. I remember being taken back by the radicalness of the quotation. It came from a piece by Marx and Engels called *The German Ideology*. It discussed the development of the productive forces said to condition the actual empirical existence of modern men, a development that inevitably renders the great mass of humanity 'property-less' and in contradiction to the existing world of wealth and culture. This serves simply, it explained, to advance the alienation of all, which is nevertheless a necessary practical premise, since without these forces of production, 'want is merely made general and along with *destitution*, the struggle for necessities, the same old crap is inevitably reproduced'.

And was not Fascism in fact a European movement, grown out of the First World War and invoking the basic need of individual peoples, the struggle of nations for basic necessities (space to live, raw materials, politics of family)? Was Fascism not a delusional ascent that unleashed, along with the forces of production, an extreme destructive power—mass murder, predatory war, brute redistributions—by generalizing lack ever further? GDR socialism was established in reaction precisely to this, a place where all the colours paled and gave way to a general grey-in-grey—all the colours except one: the unattainable red on the platforms, as a background to the slogans that hung ever higher, ever more unrealizable.

What did all this have to do with my postage stamp? It comes to my mind every time the *Führer*, this dark icon of the age, pops up once again in the media. Not an evening goes by without a compilation of TV programmes on the theme: *The Führer and the*

Blitzkrieg (martial), *Hitler and His Paladins* (sensationalist journalism), *Last Days in the Bunker* (dramaturgy of apocalypse), *Hitler's Women* (accompanied by hit songs of the time—charming). My thoughts turn to the stamp each time historians earnestly discuss a new biography of the man who took just twelve years to destroy Germany. I was born seventeen years after the end of the war; seventy-five years have passed since the suicide in the Reich Chancellery bunker, the shotgun wedding with Eva Braun. But even this author, who claimed the 'holy right to his mother tongue' for himself, is subject to the laws of copyright. Not long ago, *Mein Kampf*, the book that inspired such terror in me in my grandparents' attic, was reissued in Germany with the blessing of the federal government, under the philological supervision of a commission of historians, as if it were a classical text. And still I am startled when his name is mentioned. Where does all this come from? Every time he appears in the press, as the headline on page one of the tabloids, on the *BILD-Zeitung*, for example—'Hitler's crocodile dead in Moscow'—I see the little violet stamp again in my mind's eye.

It all started with that stamp. All the turmoil originated in that inconsequential scrap of paper. Like a poisonous butterfly, it loosened itself from the envelopes and postcards of the time and has fluttered after me throughout my life. I cannot rid myself of the nagging feeling that it will continue to cross my path in future too.

II

LANDSCAPE IN FETTERS

POSTCARD: DÜSSELDORF, 1937
REICH EXHIBITION 'WORKING PEOPLE'

Dear Mrs Cumberland!
This is the entrance to the exhibition
which is very fine indeed
and enormous!
I am thoroughly enjoying myself.
They are very kind and drive me
all over the place. Yesterday
we had been on the Autobahn
to visit the city of Essen.
That was great fun!

AUTOBAHN: Long before the word came into the world, an irresistible formula that overcame all obstacles and mobilized an entire industry, it existed as an idea. It was this idea that opened the horizon to prospects of a level expressway for motorized vehicles, connecting distant points on the map with the straightest possible line through valleys and over hills. It was first realized in Italy—not a matter of chance: this was also the country that gave birth to Futurism, after all.

Piero Puricelli, a civil engineer from Milan, had the foresight to imagine the idea long before transport planners across Europe picked it up and ran with it. It was the beginning of an enterprise that would draw all the industrialized nations across the continent into competition. The motorways of Northern Italy marked the beginning, the first sections of the route were built between Milan and Sesto, with branches to Varese, Como and Bergamo—this was where the earliest blueprints of the new *autostrada* came into being.

In German, the word 'Autobahn' first appears in 1929, in an article by the Chairman of HaFraBa, Professor Otzen. According to him, the public network of roads had nothing to do with the 'highways reserved for cars'. Instead, one should talk in terms of the Autobahn. HaFraBa was the association tasked with building the highway between the Hanseatic cities: Hamburg–Frankfurt–Basel. 'Europe is shrinking with the Autobahn', one of its representatives explained in an early memorandum. The first section financed with public money was the Cologne–Bonn link, a driving distance of barely more than 20 kilometres, completed in 1932, inaugurated by the then Lord Mayor, Konrad Adenauer, at a point when Italian Fascism was still in its year X. But the overarching momentum needed to create a pan-German company was still lacking. It would not have been possible for individual companies to have handled a project of such magnitude on their own. The economy of the Weimar Republic was only partly able to meet such demands: the various branches of industry whose collaboration would have been necessary for such a national undertaking were too caught up with their own initiatives. Notwithstanding, in the last years of democratic government in Germany, concerted efforts meant that planning had progressed apace.

Part and parcel of the myth of the Reichsautobahn is the symbolic 'ground-breaking ceremony'—it was intended to mark the beginning of a new era. With it, the new 'People's Chancellor' Adolf Hitler, in September 1933, the very year of his accession to power, styled himself as a man of action—founder of a national construction work. The *Führer* gets his hands dirty, turns fresh earth, the exertion causes a strand of hair to fall across his pale imperial brow. A powerful image—as were all of the exquisitely stage-managed images of the new regime. This action was celebrated thousands of times on postcards and special prints (and retouched to the point of abstraction as a pathetic formula) as a rallying cry against unemployment; propaganda that has endured and, in Germany, continued until well after the demise of the Thousand-Year Reich. And had not a thousand kilometres of expressway been completed only three years after construction began? 'Give Me Four Years' was the title of the huge travelling exhibition in which the new government celebrated its successes. The story of the construction of the Autobahn enjoyed pride of place in it, with huge posters presenting images of the major new construction sites, the building of the first bridges.

The Reichsautobahn was the most comprehensive construction project of National Socialism and at the same time its most enduring. The so-called 'Gauforums' (building complexes meant to symbolize Nazi might) fell into decay or were blown up after the end of the war; the outdoor theatres, or thingsteads, along with war memorials and amphitheatres built in ancient granite quarries, were discreetly demolished. Only remnants of the massive Reich Party Congress site set out over 11 square kilometres on the Zeppelin Field southwest of Nuremburg survived, and the Reich Chancellery was razed to the ground after the final battle for Berlin. What remained of the architecture of those years was either rebuilt, renamed or redeveloped beyond recognition, and scarcely stands out in the overall vista of Germany's cities. But in the eastern part of the divided Germany, as well as in the west, the motorways survived; no one gave them a thought because traffic has always continued to use them. Bridges were built that were intended to last for centuries; link roads and service stations were constructed that are as functional now as they were on their very first day. Their continued use seems to fulfil the prophecy made with characteristic pathos by Fritz Todt, Hitler's Inspector General for German Highways, who was then appointed Reich Minister for Armaments and Munitions during the war: 'These constructions are not intended for the year 1940, not the year 2000; like the cathedrals of our past they should stretch into millennia of our future.' Even foreign journalists willingly joined the chorus of admiration. A certain Stanley McClatchie, 'from the USA', writes with breathless enthusiasm about the achievements of Hitler's regime: 'In millennia to come people will look back on the Reichsautobahn as we look back now on the pyramids, the Roman roads and the Great Wall of China.'

The technical solutions discovered at this time were novel and of alarming longevity: they stood apart from architectural history to that date. People praised the marvels of modern engineering made of natural stone, steel and concrete. Not only the like-minded but also the general populace and even curious visitors coming to Germany saw in the German Autobahn a flagship work of modernism, comparable to the communal building work of the Ancient Egyptian monuments, only spread out over a huge area, and encompassing vast swathes of the landscape. A work uncoupled from any religious motivation; but still, as it were, sacred work, undertaken by a collective of toiling labourers harnessed like ants to the vision of a new technological society (Marx); or following the course of Fascism, strictly functional, created for the benefit of the ideal community of people. To support this idea there were maxims that each child could cite in his or her school essays.

'Only where Germany ends, the potholes can begin' (Adolf Hitler). Take the young Heiner Müller, for example: at school he learns his first lesson in National Socialism. He comprehends that he himself can participate in the integration into the total state. It is good that the *Führer* is building roads, my father will soon have work again, he writes. His father, first imprisoned in a concentration camp as an active Social Democrat and then freed on licence, has realized that the family will only get ahead if he calls a truce with the brown princes. He encourages his son to take a positive view of the major national job-creation scheme.

What hard going it had all been until then, how agonizingly old-fashioned and set to impede progress—*passatista*, as the Italian futurists had scornfully called it in their manifestos. But then came the bright new dawn and promised freedom of movement for the new nation of fellow Germans. *Under the stupid sun, the Greys went home. The landscape was painted on a board, and so overwrought were they that their wide-open eyes no longer sensed it becoming brighter and clearer.* Thus Carl Einstein, keen observer of avant-garde movements, in his early, visionary prose, as if he could see into the future. But wasn't technical progress in the form of the automobile in fact just the latest guise of an eternal bourgeoisie? The automobile, sold as a symbol of individual freedom, made one forget the price of conformism with increasing speed. It was the perfect instrument for the psychological conditioning of the masses, subjugating itself to every road user without exception—the driver, eyes fixed on the open road ahead and the dashboard, but also the pedestrian, the cyclist, and even animals. Did the futurists, these knights of the cockpit, with their cocktails, have any sense of where it would all lead? Did they lack the imagination to foresee what would emerge beyond all visible horizons when the last moonlight was done: the *final victory* of automotive conformism?

Mobility, the collective mania: one of the many side effects of the mammoth highway-construction project was the restriction of workers' rights. Who was inclined to champion class struggle and social justice when large construction projects were springing up left, right and centre, ensuring vast swathes of the population a good living? Wage strikes were treated as Communist-inspired plots in the Hitler state and punished with draconian measures; they were seen as flirtations with Marxism, which the goon squads of the SA soon beat out of the exhausted worker colonies. On the construction sites of the Reich, the regime also responded with full force. The Gendarmerie and the heads of political bodies immediately stepped in when things got out of hand. And even those who did not own a car were soon persuaded by the idea of general progress. Soon there would be a KdF (or Strength through Joy) car for everyone (later called the Volkswagen), a black tin can in the shape of a pretzel, hot off the German production lines, and affordable even for the working class, at a fixed price of 1,000 Reichsmark, a down payment was sufficient. Even my grandfather, the assistant policeman, had already paid a deposit (which he never saw again). A passenger car for the whole family, a container for transporting the smallest cell of the state to all corners of the country, travelling on the precisely planned, comfortable concrete ribbons which would connect grandchildren and their obscure relations the length and breadth of greater Germany: the farmer and the hereditary aunt, the city dweller and the secluded spa town in the Thuringian Forest, the 'brown' student and his pious parents at home and vice versa.

Already in 1933 Heinrich Mann harbours no illusions about the real reasons for the dictator's ambitious Autobahn project:

> The regime has indeed taken over the plan to build a highway directly from Berlin to Milan with luxury hotels the length of the route. The plan is so little in tune with the true economic situation that it offends, as it were, against decency. The truth of the matter is this: the dictator is very keen on driving and does not like being on foot, although that might in fact do him some good and clear his head a little. Besides, another point in its favour is that the intended route would be conspicuous proof of the close link between the two Fascist movements. At the root of every practical measure and even the automobile traffic one should look for the ruthless determination of a regime that wishes to endure.

Thousands of kilometres of nature structurally integrated into the project, with the inclusion of native landscapes *from the Meuse to the Memel, from the Adige to the Belt*, as the Deutschlandlied went, a nation-spanning work that spoke for itself. Rarely have the seeds of Nazi propaganda shot up as successfully as in the construction of the Autobahn. The new state put out the call and those seeking work, who had only recently been on unemployment stamps, were at once integrated into the 'German Labour Front' and came pouring onto the new construction sites from the North Sea to the Bavarian Alps. The Autobahn was the work of many thousands of willing helpers, a dream project of totalitarian planning. What did it matter that none of those caught up into the whirlwind could ever feel free, that everything was only a postponement, preparation for the next planned war of revenge, for which the motorways were needed as a means of rapid troop deployment, something which never came to pass in the end, because—unlike today—the German railway fulfilled this task much more efficiently.

Across the country, temporary settlements for the gangs of workers, dubbed Reich Labour Camps, sprang up overnight. Men and women were separated. This was the crucial division in the Third Reich (*he* at work with a pneumatic drill, *she* in the maternity home at the cost of the state; then later *he* with a machine gun, *she* on the assembly line of the munitions factory): a world of work in which gender segregation sealed what would not change until the final victory. In the UFA film palaces, meanwhile, the myth was propagated in the flights of fancy of the silver screen. *With these words, from the furthest horizon the sun stretched its fiery, trembling steering wheel towards us* (Filippo Tommaso Marinetti, *Let's Kill the Moonlight*).

'For the Autobahn *is* aesthetics', claims Friedrich Kittler in a visionary essay. 'For motorized vehicles', the official work *Constructions of the Movement* explains in 1937, 'the Motorways of the Reich embody arteries: they are not interlopers in the landscape, but a harmonious part of the scenery.' The reason for this was rather less public: unlike the autostrada or the autoroute, the Autobahn avoided any 'unnecessarily deep' embankment which it would need to 'cut out of the landscape'. As Fritz Todt establishes based on his constant contact with the army: 'the Autobahn should not become a mouse trap from which military vehicles could not escape.' And in this way peacetime planning does excellent service for Hans Kammler's rocket companies, which even at the end, under the hail of Allied bombs, are chasing across the motorways to propel V2s towards London and into World War X+1.

The Reichsautobahn was sold as a national work of construction, although, in truth, the propaganda value was, from the very start, more important than the economic use. 'Motor highways and dried-up Pontine marshes are the Potemkin villages of totalitarian dictatorships', declares Siegfried Kracauer, recognizing the true impetus for mobilization inherent in such Fascist enterprises. The Reichsautobahn was the result of a highly organized collaboration between engineers, architects, craftsmen and landscape designers, executed by teams of thousands of workers, who were removed from the streets with the promise of pitiful daily wages. Later, after the war had really begun, they were followed by an army of forced labourers, deported from all over subjugated Europe, true slaves who could only dream of fair pay.

In the end, however, the RAB or Reichsautobahn was the only legacy of the Third Reich that was truly beneficial to those who came after. Something had been created that did not have to be destroyed in shame—and could indeed be extended with an eye firmly to the future. Thanks to the motorway network, Germany could move seamlessly towards the years of the economic miracle— it was a guarantee of the continued success of German business. The demand was high, indeed excessive: the same people, if they had survived, set straight back to work again. The notion that roads were to be regarded as a work of art had already been forgotten and now people concentrated on the engineering problems that lay ahead. People had no time for the 'car as a bridge to the landscape', as it was dubbed in 'Nazi-German', and simply built instead on what their hardworking predecessors had left behind. To be fair, they likely thought they had been deluded, but, on the other hand, one could build visual blinds that would help block out the din of the 'Carry on Regardless' mindset. A question mark was not a symbol that appeared in the traffic regulations—and even they could be taken over almost unchanged.

In June 1933, a law establishing a company for the Reichsautobahn was passed and parliament, which had already been forcibly brought into line with Nazi policy, functioned as smoothly as ever in this respect. Party Member Fritz Todt was appointed Inspector General for German Highways: the name, Todt—like Tod or death—a coincidence, and yet also a programmatic threat. This was the new economic policy: the state awarded contracts; and commissioners with far-reaching powers ensured their fulfilment. Resistance was not expected. Todt, an old-school engineer at heart, developed the concept of 'line management', a basic idea that was subsequently easily transferrable to other administrative areas— for example, the one which, in the wake of the intensified racial ideology, was responsible for the 'final solution' of the Jewish question. 'Parallel line management' of all the participating services was the magic formula that SS-Obergruppenführer Reinhard Heydrich scribbled on a notepad during the Wannsee conference, as the key to coordinating the secret extermination plan, the physical extinction of all European Jews.

Pursuing the 'German rationalization' only became possible with the advent of the planned economy in the *Führer*-state. It was the introduction of norms and standardization, to stick with the Nationalist Socialist technical jargon, that led to a breakthrough across the entire work front. 'The obligation to increase productivity across all areas of human activity is the object of our age.' Though that only truly came into force with the post-war economy of the German nation, the monumental work of reconstruction that must have made the Allies as uneasy as the drive to modernization of the Third Reich.

There was the 'Reich Centre for Regional Planning'; it was followed by the 'Reich Planning Association', and both were preceded by the 'Society for the Preparation of Reich Planning and Regional Planning', or GEZUVOR—music to the ears of an administrative bureaucracy that had survived all the political systems in Germany. Everything starts small but can quickly become large and end up encompassing an entire country. At first there were only sketches, but the sketches soon became norms—long before the challenging, intrepid bridge constructions, the more than a hundred motorway intersections with their distribution lanes all the way along the interconnected routes and connecting ramps.

'Now we turn the radio on
From the loudspeakers hear the song:
Wir fahr'n auf der Autobahn'

sang the West German electropop band Kraftwerk to the new
sound of the synthesizer, decades later, when everything had
become an orderly routine. At this point though, the motorway-
mania continued unabated, thanks to an unprecedented wave of
mobilization in the wake of the economic miracle. The 'motorization mania' as it was called by Marxist economic historians, continued beyond National Socialism. Post-war Germany had long
since picked up speed again, as quick to build as to forget. *The highway is a grey band, green edge, white lines* (Kraftwerk). By the 1980s
the whole thing was already a matter of course, part of the normal
reality of life in West Germany, when in the summer, following the
general surge, you headed south with the car radio playing the hit
'Voyage, Voyage' by the French singer Desireless on an endless
loop. At that time, the motorway was like a promise of future times,
which grew ever larger with each legislative term, and one asked
nothing more of the government than that tax revenues flowed
straight into highway construction and that everything would pro-
ceed without obstacle from now on and forever more. People of all
ages and classes now spent more and more time in their private
cars, which meant that certain transport hubs were often over-
loaded, especially at rush hour. Traffic jams became a permanent
state of affairs, especially in the holiday season, when everyone
departed at the same moment, and stoically adjusted to the
inevitable. Entire families were now on the motorway and, if the
worst should happen, would be completely wiped out in a moment
of inattention. What did Annie Ernaux write in her narrative
chronicle *The Years*?

We were nothing but a gaze behind the windscreen transparent to the end of the moving horizon, an immense, fragile consciousness that filled inner space, if not the entire world beyond it. All it would take, we sometimes told ourselves, was for a tyre to explode or an obstacle to appear on the road, as in Claude Sautet's *The Things of Life*, for this consciousness to vanish for ever.

As early as the spring of 1933, the idea of a two-lane highway exclusively for motorized vehicles, with separate lanes for oncoming traffic had been aired. The carriageways were to be divided by a green strip providing a central reservation, and motorists shielded from the glare of oncoming traffic at night. The new cross-section was a lane width of 3.75 metres, the German standard: to this very day it is the basis of motorway construction. Likewise, the enclosure of the carriageways with fixed sidings, supplemented, if necessary, by a hard shoulder with the same immaculate concrete surface. A method of building the highways with a transverse gradient or camber soon became the norm, because it was already clear, on account of the centrifugal forces, that on some sections of the route the vehicles would be leaning at an angle, like the racing cars at the Nürburgring racing track and on the AVUS, the Berlin race-track.

The first uniform standard cross-section of the motorway of the German Reich was decreed by the head office of the Reichsautobahn in January 1934: standard cross-section 23, that is two carriageways, each 7.50 metres wide. The distance was later expanded. From May 1935, a standard cross-section of a total of 24 metres was applied across the Reich and was put into force on just over three-quarters of all motorway routes. The road network now

provided for three links from north to south and three east to west. The hubs, spread throughout the Reich, were Hamburg, Stettin, Berlin, Breslau and Hildesheim; Cologne, Frankfurt, Stuttgart, Nuremberg, Dessau and Munich were added later. They were to be 'highways without obstacle', even the crash barriers along the side of the motorway had already been provided for. Road construction took over the whole of Germany as if it were a new yet unknown continent, all in accordance with a policy of integration into the landscape. The highway should adapt to the terrain, not the other way around. Conservation of nature was paramount in a country where a certain percentage of its inhabitants, following recent racial doctrine, were branded as vermin and condemned to extinction. It was vital to preserve the essential character of the Volk, and of the geographical landscape, by technical means: for example, the experience of space when passing through forest areas. 'Especially when passing through a forest', a highway planner writes in a paper for the magazine *Die Straße*, 'it is helpful if the driver cannot see the end of the forest as soon as he enters it, but, rather, the curve in the road should allow the view of the exit to appear only shortly before leaving the forest, so that the experience of the forest is extended.'

Like other architectural showpieces of the Third Reich, such as the Ordensburg fortresses picturesquely placed on plateaus or before mountainous backdrops, and visible from far and wide, the Reichsautobahn was consciously positioned in the landscape. German order prevailed here, too: the sections of the route were divided into three classes. Class 1 was the lowland routes without significant obstacles, and a maximum gradient of 4 percent; Class 2 encompassed mountainous terrain; and Class 3 the extended stretches in higher mountain regions. Here the driver went uphill and down in a series of exhilarating curves, built always with the unobstructed panoramas in mind. The road was made to adapt to the alpine conditions by means of bridges and tunnels in order to accentuate only the best aspects of the landscape. In the same way the painters of the time celebrated the scenery in the style of 'New Sobriety' with echoes of Romanticism, so the poets were encouraged to collect sentimental verses celebrating their native soil in Echtermeyer, the famous anthology of German folk poetry. How inspiring the subject matter proved is demonstrated by the fact that among open-air painters a new, distinct genre began to develop: that of motorway landscapes.

But even today's motorist will struggle to escape the directorial interventions of the planners of that time. Breath-taking curves of moulded concrete were constructed, created by nameless engineers: the phantasmagoria of a rampant modernity. There were far-reaching transitional arcs—*clothoids*—curves in which the curvature is proportional to the length of their arc to the place where they met on the level ground. Who would have thought that baroque geometry and Euler spirals would one day combine to create the perfect driving experience? That graphs would become sensations, that curves calculated in excruciating mathematics lessons would one day turn into bodily experiences of speed and exhilaration. Who could have dreamed that one day you would be sitting at the wheel and feel the most elegant curves press into your very spine with merely a touch of the steering wheel?

Like an opera stage, it all became a matter of comprehensively imagined staging and powerful visual scenography. The manuals of the motorway builders contained the components of a new composition theory for navigable space. There was talk of route-mapping, of expansion of the carriageway, of extending the central reservation, of low and high kerb stones. The issue of rounding off the embankment was also discussed as a precautionary measure. The ramps onto and off the carriageway were the subject of specialized calculations, concerning smooth transitions or torsion. All possible corollaries were considered: planted areas to reduce glare, green verges. Even the ancient single lime tree was generously included *in memoriam* Franz Schubert. The technicians' compromise: the preservation of the single tree in the middle of the central reservation. Out of all this came the exemplary image of a German motorway. In the words of the most senior road-planner Fritz Todt: 'The traveller should not simply use the roads to get from one place to another as quickly as possible, but also to experience and enjoy the beauties of the country.' It was about tailoring the routes to accentuate important beauty spots such as church towers, ruined

castles, picturesque groves of trees. Car parks situated at higher altitude should give out on Romantic vistas. The example par excellence was the establishment of the Aachen–Cologne route, with Cologne Cathedral already visible in the distance from the start as destination and enticing end point.

The central reservation too was a German invention that emerged at this time, as a safety measure that arrived in parallel with the idea of adjacent carriageways carrying traffic in opposite directions. And it is still in operation to this day. If someone comes off the road they can still be caught by the crash barrier. In a eulogy for the German road supremo Fritz Todt, who had been killed in an aeroplane crash, the architect and Armament Minister Albert Speer waxed lyrical about the 'tracking' of the new roads, a technical term that had such a *classy* ring to it (a fashionable Nazi term of the time) that the technicians' mouths watered.

Gigantic bridges were built across the valleys, *in bold, rousing curves*. The astonishing multiple-arch constructions were a welcome challenge for the engineers. Thus, as the cinema newsreel proclaimed, the 'largest Reichsautobahn bridge in the world' came into being at this time, spanning the Mulde valley near Siebenlehn, in Saxony. Rhetoric drenched in high pathos celebrating the conquest of nature, in sound and image. Or the bridge over the Teufelstal valley on the Thuringian motorway between Stadtroda and Hermsdorf, the Lautertal Bridge at Kaiserslautern and in Bavaria the Mangfall Bridge on the short section of road between Munich and the border—each a triumph over material reality. A triumph too over the yielding softness of nature, figured as a female and brought to submission by the hands of hardworking men over the course of thousands of shifts.

And then the cities, too, had to be brought into the network. Every major town along the various routes was still an island needing to be connected to the traffic system. A particular challenge to the directorial ingenuity of the planners was the entrance to a given city: the key was to design the approach in terms of perspective, in the grand style—of course. Several of these cities had been declared pearls in the crown of German culture, like the old town of Dresden in the Elbe valley, to which the *Führer* personally promised to give a new National Socialist incarnation. Hitler's chosen cities, the so-called *Führerstädte*, also included Hamburg, 'Capital of German Shipping', and Munich, 'Capital of The Movement', as well as Berlin, which had been slumbering in obscurity for so long and had now been awakened as 'The World Capital of Germania'. 'Movement' was the buzzword of the hour: one that promised to align all the dynamic forces—from politics to transport technology, industry and rearmament for war. An entire country was on the move, the state summoned its populace to the construction sites, the parade grounds and soon to the barracks for the next act in the opera. *Gesamtkunstwerk* Deutschland. A prime example of the new aesthetic of grandiosity was the entrance to Mannheim, completed in 1935, including the no less magnificent Rhine-Neckar arena with white towers at the entrance, emblazoned with the imperial eagle, along with capital letters on the grass spelling out: Reichsautobahn.

Reichsautobahn. Einfahrt in Mannheim.

Overnight, the Autobahn had become the German trademark, a synonym like Selters for mineral water, Juno for cigarettes or Continental, the market-leader in the car tyre industry at the time. Hundreds of patents arising during the motorway construction were filed within a few years—many are still valid to this day, deposited in the German patent office in Munich.

Exact measurements had proved 'that road surfaces manufactured in this way are level to within one millimetre.' On top of the original concrete surface, originally interspersed with wooden planks placed vertically as a grouting board, came a second layer. Only sand and gravel were used for this, natural materials, sufficiently water-permeable, free of soluble components and thus immune to the damage caused by changing weather conditions. Before long, this mammoth construction work caused more earth to be excavated than the construction of the Panama and Suez Canals combined, as stated in the declamatory weekly newsreel that pedalled one exorbitant exaggeration after the next. Once the substructure had been rolled flat, came an application of oil paper over the entire surface to insulate the concrete from the damp substrate. The next layer of concrete was then applied using a hopper. The man operating this, a qualified specialist, ensured the even distribution of the concrete. After that, the motor once again sprang into action to level the surface by means of numerous small tamping motions. Meanwhile the giant concrete mixers (with a capacity of 1,500 litres) drove back and forth, and gravel and cement were fetched on special tipper trucks. The boards were there to prevent faults in the concrete at high temperatures. From a moving operating platform, the remaining contraction joints were then sanded clean by hand and later filled with hemp and asphalt. This resulted in the narrow joints characteristic of the Reichsautobahn. 'So that cars driving at speed do not suffer vibrations as they travel over the joints.' By this point, the linguistic mechanization of life, which began during the First World War and the years of the Weimar Republic, was already well advanced. Along with language, daily life had long since 'toed the line' under the constraints of a modern civilization governed by the technology of traffic.

As a child the noise when one drove over these joints in the road surface became such a familiar bodily sensation that I can recall it at any time, just by closing my eyes. On the annual trips to Thuringia to visit my grandparents and up to the Baltic Sea on summer holidays it was a reliable companion. A gentle, rumbling rhythm that seemed to echo in your head and make you sleepy straightaway, until your eyes closed, and you sank into a deep motorway slumber. It was not until many kilometres later that you were suddenly jolted awake and saw Ettersberg on the right, on a distant sand-coloured hill, and the tall bell tower monument of the former concentration camp Buchenwald; or to the left, just before the turnoff to Gotha, the 'Drei Gleichen', or Three Brothers, a series of ruins of medieval castles, which each time we spotted them gave our father at the wheel the opportunity to tell us all the legends associated with them, told in turn to him by his grandfather during his childhood in Thuringia. And while he was telling the stories, long after the interchange at Hermsdorf and the Saale valley Bridge at Jena, just beyond Wandersleben, I would finally nod off.

Almost everything had been thought of in the construction of the Reichsautobahn. The transverse-joints were staggered unevenly, according to precise calculations, so the vehicle vibrations did not make the passengers feel sick, like the boat swings at Dresden's Vogelwiese meadow which, having tried them once, I made sure to avoid every time I visited the fair.

Civil engineers and concrete experts had collaborated to dis-cover a perfect formula for connecting the base layer, upper layer and expansion joints of the motorway so skilfully that driving was a matter of a perfect gliding motion. The same caution was exercised with bridges. For example, the steel superstructure was placed on point rocker bearings, using a new type of steel (ST 52). 'Works of *lasting eternal value*' were created as they were called in the schmaltzy, false Nazi German.

The notebook of a Jewish philologist had alerted me to the distorted German of those years. It had fallen into my hands in a Dresden antiquarian bookshop, which was on my way to school: Victor Klemperer's *LTI. The Language of the Third Reich* (Lingua Tertii Imperii). One example among many of the ruined grammar of the time was Hitler's speeches, in which the power of language came less to the fore than the violence done to language. From a speech to Berlin workers on 1 May: 'I will have no greater source of pride in my life than being able to say at the end of my days: *I have conquered the German Reich for the German worker!*'

The suspicion that there was also something wrong with the language of my school days, the German of the Workers' and Peasants' State, was substantiated by my own reading. 'The Third Reich speaks with a terrible uniformity in all its utterances and legacies: in the unbounded exhibitionism of its grandiose architecture and through its ruins . . . through its motorways and mass graves. All of this is the language of the Third Reich.' From this study I learnt that verbs such as *ankurbeln* (crank up, boost) and *spuren* (keep on track) that were brand new then, though ubiquitous now, originated in the technical vocabulary of the automobile industry, and had quickly penetrated everyday language before the propaganda specialists of the Third Reich began to use them in an inflationary way and for their own purposes. At the time, it struck me how quickly technical terms find their way into all areas of human existence and take hold of everyday life: 'Everything is back on track (*Es spurt schon wieder*). (I had this specialist term from the field of automobile construction explained to me: the wheels on the vehicle stay on the right track),' Victor Klemperer wrote in his notebook.

And why is everything on the right track in the Third Reich with its rousing four-year economic plans? Because everyone, thanks to all-round organization, was 'working at full capacity' (*voll ausgelastet*). And the turn of phrase 'at full capacity', a favourite expression of Goebbels at the time, was an incursion from the language of technology into the everyday language of the little people. Only this incursion seemed less aggressive than the motor running at full tilt. But look, it turned out that human shoulders could be used to capacity in the same way 'like any other load-bearing structure'.

Such a phrase pinpointed the interface between human and Autobahn, the connection between technological changes to the environment and linguistic formatting. Who today honours the thousands of bodies ground down during the construction work that built by dint of force what everyone was happy to use afterwards? Who is still aware of the shifts in vocabulary that came with such progress, the prime movers under the political diktat and their cost to the individual? It was men, miserable, exhausted wretches for the most part, who took on the Babylonian construction, day labourers from the great army of the unemployed, who at that time gave the only thing they had to give, their declining labour power.

As new sections of the route began to emerge, labour camps were set up alongside, often in the most makeshift conditions, in which voluntary workers, far from their families, operated under military discipline, kept in check by Party supervisors, should their class consciousness ever raise its head. Troublemakers and ringleaders were immediately neutralized—*ausgeschaltet* as the Nazi jargon of the time had it. This was the responsibility of a designated department of the Reich Labour Service, later also the Gestapo. Here, as in any other social sphere, infiltration of such groups by informers was meant to stem the rot. But still, the problems never abated. Illnesses brought on by exhaustion were the rule, accidents at work as a result of stress, fatigue and lack of training. Over the course of the first five years of construction, one statistic confirms that for every six kilometres of motorway completed, there was at least one fatally injured worker.

Women were excluded from the road construction as a matter of principle. Using them would have contradicted the new biopolitics, the structure of gender relations based on breeding potential: the woman at the stove and those who distinguished themselves in childbearing awarded the 'Mother's Cross', because the state required children for the war effort and the conquest of new territories. That was until planning stalled with the momentum of the War. Then female forced labourers from the subjugated eastern territories (and only from there) had to make up for the shortfall of male workers. Until then, however, the strict organization of the everyday life of those in the business of breeding was in operation, a programme so closely supervised that there was no room for wage disputes and the struggle for emancipation. Female engineers in the planning office, female executives in the industrial workforce? Completely unthinkable: at best, women served as secretaries in the various control rooms, or assistants in the chain of command, in the ministries involved, women as shorthand typists, nicknamed 'typing pool totty', or in official German, 'typewriter personnel', in the offices of the Reichsautobahn planners.

The organization of work under National Socialism was based on strict gender segregation. In maintaining the worker's 'contradiction in himself' (Wilhelm Reich), the Hitler movement had done quite a job. Their breeding ground was narrowly conservative life, petty-bourgeois domestic culture, the longing of a worker to set up a modest life for himself and his own within the scope allowed by his fixed wage. In addition, the need for festivals and family holidays in the rota of working weeks and organized trips within the framework of the KdF or 'Strength through Joy' programme, which even included subsidized trips abroad on the special 'strength-buses' and cruise ship tours to Spain and Norway, allocated randomly like a People's Lottery. From his distant Californian shores, Thomas Mann called it 'shipping herds of disenfranchised workers to beautiful locations'.

In the evening dress worn by workers at the National Socialist office party, in the familiar rituals of beer drinking, wrote Wilhelm Reich, lay more truth about the reactionary structure of the workers' lives than in hundreds of articles of the once-proud Communist press. The compulsion to develop technology kept everyone in check. The exemplary model for this was construction of the Autobahn, staged as a heroic 'work battle'. If surveys had been permitted at the time, the psychologist would undoubtedly have found his theory of alignment with the repressive sexual morality of the petty bourgeoisie confirmed. The highway builder was the diligent onanist in the service of the *Führer*'s state, dreaming of home leave on his camp bed in the labour camp after a long day's work. Or of meeting his *sweetheart* at the cinema or looking forward to the family outing with the faithful little wife who was looking after the children at home. There were now offices for everything: the 'Office for the Beauty of Labour' (an organization under the umbrella of the German Labour Front or DAF) provided for the expansion of accommodation, the department dubbed 'Special Initiative for the Imperial Highways' within the 'Office for Leisure Time' took care of evening activities in the form of film evenings, lectures and concerts. After achieving the daily set work norms, the men were lulled with comedies; beloved actors Heinz Rühmann and Ilse Werner could be relied on to create a good mood. The cheap labour supplied by the reserve army of the unemployed was replaced after 1935 by the so-called spade squads of the Reich Labour Service. They were the harbingers of the future war economy. Tightly organized, in paramilitary style they had only to obey the order to go into action.

Maybe that was how it was: men are creatures that build roads, machines and motor cars, in which they hope one day to head into the sunset with the woman of their dreams—with this dream in mind they accept all the hardships and even their transformation into a coolie. Thousands of Myrmidons were caught up in the system, without any thought of uprising or revolutionary struggle. Not only the unemployed from all walks of life, who were set to work overnight, but also many of the skilled civil engineers and unskilled construction labourers were brought to the very limit of their strength by years of malnutrition. Popularly, people spoke of a kind of 'Foreign Legion'. The workers saw themselves as exploited welfare recipients. The extreme workload, primitive accommodation, the resulting high level of sickness and pitiful wages quickly led to the realization that they had fallen into a trap. But by then it was too late, Germany had voted, and every single person was dependent on the great construction sites of the Reich for better or worse. Or, as the leader of the German Labour Front, Robert Ley, announced with remarkable candour: 'We won't let anyone go, and when it's all over the Labour Front will take up the individual again and again, and won't let go of them until the grave, however they struggle against it.'

This spelt the end for any kind of proletarian resistance. The worker in motorway construction or the arms industry, the steel worker or the coal miner in the 'Hermann Göring' plant, all these stood at the end of the collective development. Just as ribbons of asphalt and marvellous bridges were popping up all over German soil, Wilhelm Reich, the psychologist of the masses summarized thus: 'Disappointment in Social Democracy accompanied by the contradiction between impoverishment and conservative thinking must lead straight to Fascism.'

ASPHALT was the word that, according to the National Socialist dogma, was considered a synonym for the hated, unnatural modernity, that was denounced, on the one hand, but which was inexorably advanced as a vital technical development, on the other. The 'asphalt man' had been a slogan of the right in the party infighting of the Weimar Republic. It referred not only to the city dweller but also to the intellectual elite tout court, the coffeehouse man of letters, the 'cultural Bolshevik'. In his pamphlet *Der Mythus des 20. Jahrhunderts* (The Myth of the Twentieth Century) Alfred Rosenberg, chief ideologue of the Nazi Party, also spoke of the labour movement as the *rising asphalt humanity of the world's megalopolis with all the wretched refuse of Asia.* According to this doctrine, however, the word 'refuse' designated none other than the Jew, universal outsider, the very essence of the uprooted person, belonging

Blick v. d. Reichsautobahn in's Dresdner Elbtal

to a community that, according to accepted racial sociology at the time, embodied all that was un-German, every evil of alienation, and had like a 'parasite' spread across Europe and America, thanks in no small part to the new transport routes now available to the born nomad of the world in his necessary mobility. The German worker, on the other hand, the domesticated wage slave cured of all proletarian ambitions, who hauled the bitumen mixture into the cities as part of the road construction programmes and commanded the steamroller, had unavoidably found himself falling in with the project of the racial ideologues. As a non-Jew, he had gone along with the idea of being a member of the master race, meaning that if he had nothing else, he at least had this: his Aryanism. Replacing class hatred with racial hatred was the easiest sleight of hand of the century. Marxism as the emancipation of the individual ousted by the idea of the rise of the masses in Fascism. He was enmeshed with hide and hair, in the *German national community*, and there was no way out. All the *Streets of the Führer* led only to war.

Contradictions wherever you looked. This was also noticed by someone like the philosopher Martin Heidegger, who at the time saw himself as adviser to the tyrants following the model of Plato. In his Freiburg speech on the occasion of his appointment as rector of the university there, he welcomed the 'National Socialist Revolution' and welcomed the *Führer*-principle as the fulfilment of true democracy. What did the author of *Der Feldweg* (The Fieldpath) know about the bureaucracy of the employment offices? What of the distress of the millions forced to work and later to war? There is much talk of machinations, miserable concoctions, and the processes of power in his *Black Notebooks*, his private records from 1939–41. '"Powerful" now signifies "gigantic", but never means "sovereign"—a "powerful" chimney in a factory . . . .' This contemplator of origins was, as a philosopher, purely fixated on language—and so he missed the point of a form of mastery that operated via mass media and rested on linguistic manipulation so new and overwhelming that it completely captivated him. He did not see through it and recognize it as the essence of totalitarian power relations; believing instead that he could parry it with language, a language of his own based on linguistic analysis of the origins of words. The few who knew anything about it, critical spirits like Walter Benjamin, Siegfried Kracauer, Hannah Arendt, Wilhelm Reich or Carl Einstein had by that time long since been driven into exile, and were agitating far from Germany, all of them fighting a lost cause.

This was no coincidence either: no sooner was construction of the Autobahn in full swing than a driving ban was issued for the Jewish section of the population. This was prompted by an incident in Paris. In an act of desperation, the seventeen-year-old Herschel Grynszpan, a German-Polish Jew, shoots the diplomat Ernst von Rath, outraged by the forced deportation of his family by German authorities. Heinrich Himmler, in his capacity as Chief of Police, then takes the decision: the Jews have been using 'the imperial highways built by German workers' hands', they have forfeited their rights as road users. The surrender of their driving licence was just one of many compulsory measures enforced against the Jewish minority after the Nuremberg laws came into force.

So it was that the Professor of Romance Languages Victor Klemperer, after all other indignities heaped upon him, also suffered this. After losing his University chair, Klemperer and his wife had managed to gain a little private freedom by buying a car. Life in forced retirement, with increasingly scarce resources and continued arbitrary acts of intimidation was made a little brighter by being able to make excursions to the local surroundings of Saxony and once even to the Reich capital Berlin. They treated themselves to a tour of the Giant Mountains, in the late summer of 1937; also 'a coastal drive and a visit to the cities of the Hanseatic League', meaning that they were among the first users of the new motorways. An almost childlike enthusiasm for technology had taken hold of the scholar. Klemperer's diary is full of euphoric observations about every aspect of the automobile. 'The car, the car above all, it has caught our imagination utterly.' But now this last joy was taken from them. Since he was the only one in possession of a driving licence, and not his 'Aryan' wife, this meant that the whole business was at an end. '*Withdrawal of the Driving License from All Jews.* The ban has hit us exceedingly hard.'

'Yesterday Braunschweig. Back at midnight. The Reichsautobahn—it is wonderfully fast! You can drive at a hell of a tempo.' This is what Gottfried Benn writes on a postcard from Hanover to his lover in Berlin, Elinor Büller, in March 1937. He had been travelling in a chauffeured service car, in his capacity as army medical inspector, on what is now the A2. The speed had lifted his spirits. Aha, if only the lady in question, desired with such erotic intensity at the weekend, could zip over to him just as quickly. Sometimes he must take the fast train to Berlin, sometimes she visits the lonely lodger at his place. It puts one in mind of the bitter words of Klaus Mann, who had written in exile about his former idol: 'Now he's stuck as a sullen medical officer in Hanover.' Or more pointedly still, in the tone of one cursing the renegade: 'One isn't transferred to Hanover, but to hell.' For it was nigh impossible to make amends for the story of the poet Benn's dalliance with the brown philistines, from whom someone like him would otherwise have received a publication ban. And so, he often sat alone drinking beer in one of the city's bars, while the love nest remained for the most part cold. Vital for upholding their long-distance relationship were the regular letters exchanging sweet nothings, but the Autobahn never played a role, for the simple reason that Benn did not possess a driving license.

No sooner were the first sections of the Reichsautobahn put into service than numerous serious accidents occurred: vehicles crashing into parking trucks, for example. This made it necessary to widen the fortified hard shoulder adjacent to the road. The significant increase in volume of heavy goods traffic, especially in the south of Germany, and frequent necessity of overtaking long-distance freight lorries that accompanied it meant that an additional fast lane was required. The expansion of the roads raced ahead of the production capacity of the car industry. It was only gradually that the promised motorization of the masses got underway, with the aim of overcoming the idea of the automobile as a luxury commodity for the elite and making the commercial car available to all. The prematurely heralded equality of all road users was still a long way off. After all, Germany was not America where the tycoon Henry Ford, whom Hitler revered along with aviator Charles Lindbergh, had switched motor-car production to assembly-line manufacture. His Ford Model-T flew off the production line millions at a time, it was the best-selling car in the world.

Gottfried Benn, on the other hand, had already noted, and not without sarcasm, what the spirit of technology had done to nature. In his 1927 story 'Urgesicht' (Primal Vision), he had passed judgement on the new age: 'It ripped foundlings from the fields and spewed forth community blocks from its bowels, it smeared forests with concrete for a humanity engaged in multiplication.' In just a few words he captures the image of a complete transformation of the landscape. Even though the poet was certainly not one who longed nostalgically for the return to an idyll of unspoilt nature, he had long since grasped the way the wind was blowing.

Those who drove on the Reichsautobahn in the early years ploughed a lonely furrow, in contemplative calm. For hundreds of kilometres nothing but pristine concrete, sealed-off meadows, a landscape in fetters, cut across in straight lines or hyperbolae. On advertising postcards, vehicles often had to be inserted into the picture afterwards to create the impression of traffic. Desert tracks heading into nowhere, with pylons on the horizon, constructions in the spirit of abstract art, that belied all the homeland romanticism conjured by German administrators.

In the area of the Rhine–Main route near Frankfurt, where traffic was most dense, a combination of trucks, KdF buses and numerous private cars provide the standard popular image. Above them, a Zeppelin dramatically launches into the sky, the hangar stands dark in the background like the terminal for an unrealized future. Chimeras like this drove the fantasies of the Reichsautobahn planners, science fiction was in the air. The motorway landscape was thought to be educating a new type of human being, true to the prevailing blood-and-earth ideology. Otto Kurz, in *Future Images of the Landscape and the Reichsautobahn*:

> It is therefore just as necessary to keep our landscape pure and clean and to preserve its character in the way that has long since been taken for granted for blood, that is, for a humanity of racially impeccable pedigree. Landscape design must therefore stand alongside the politics of race; both point and pave the way to the development of our people over the next centuries.

Everything revolved around creating the overall impression of *Heimat*, the phantasm of an organic architecture. Thus, on the shores of Lake Chiemsee, a motorway service station complex had been built; Hitler, the thwarted landscape painter, personally intervened in the designs. He demanded that the architects imitate the native design of the Alpine region. Later, on his trips to Obersalzberg, he enjoyed planning a stopover there and paying a visit to the establishment, designed to look like an Alpine country house with a large dining room divided with marble columns from Ruhpolding. The complex still stands today, and is listed.

Another thing to have survived is the so-called AVUS (Automobile Traffic and Training Road), in Berlin, with which it all began. It was the first stretch of road exclusively for vehicles in Germany, a kind of vehicular appendix on the outskirts of the city. Until 1940, it served as a racing track for the legendary Mercedes Silver Arrow speedsters and sports cars emerging out of domestic production. However, the AVUS was also a test track in other respects. It was during its ongoing development that the characteristic smooth fixed road surface was developed, an entirely new tar and concrete blend that made the motorway construction possible on a large scale.

Berliners knew the long loop with its two 8-kilometre sides and its wide double carriageway through the Grunewald, mainly as the venue for motorcycle road championships, where races were held for the German Grand Prix. The covered grandstands still stand there like forgotten umbrellas after Europe's last rain, not far from the radio tower and the imperial sports field site (Olympiad 1936). How often we would pass them on the way out of town, setting off towards the old West German states, to the Ruhr or to Munich, 600 kilometres away. We, this was the collective 'we' that dispersed on the highways and scattered right across the country—people who were trying to get out, out on the wings of the highway. By Dreilinden at the latest, the former checkpoint at the former border, where even in the 1990s, young women in jeans or light skirts, or men with heavy backpacks would loiter in the hope of a ride, you breathed a sigh of relief and put your foot down, because there were still several hours of driving ahead of you. Now began the grumbling at the wheel. Germany, blasted country, so vast that you had to divide the travel time between boredom and euphoria, feelings that gripped all who vanquished this landmass at more than a hundred kilometres per hour—and gripped them anew every time.

The Germans, at least the privileged few who had their own car in the Third Reich, were not able to enjoy the comfort of the new overland roads for long. As early as 1 January 1942, the expansion of the Reichsautobahn was discontinued on account of the war. A month later, all private journeys by motorcar were banned to save fuel for the war effort. Now the war had effectively side-lined the project. During the final years of hostilities, the motorways, in their ghostly emptiness, must have looked like speedway tracks across the salt flats of Utah—just a mirage in the summer heat. During the Allied attacks on targets important for the war effort, they were mostly spared, although the military had feared that their bright shimmering concrete surfaces could serve the bombers as land-marks—highly visible patterns criss-crossing the enemy soil. Unlike the railway lines, they were hardly ever used as supply lines and were usually repaired quickly, in the event that occasional bombers unloaded their cargo onto them during the return flight.

In the end, only the imposing motorway ruins, scattered through-out the Reich, testified to the ambitious project: shorter sections between Fulda and Würzburg, between Hamm and Warburg, the longest was the surviving fragment of motorway from Vienna via Brno to Wroclaw. Here, for the last time, planners applied what they had learnt from previous stages of construction. A small tri-umph of art on the fringes: in his perspective drawings, a Viennese landscape painter had used curved lines to show how the terrain could be harmoniously embedded in what was left of the suppos-edly untouched natural surroundings, and this according to the characteristics of the different administrative districts of Germany. According to Otto Kurz, the Reichsautobahn should help 'to make it easier for one tribe to get to know and appreciate another's idiosyncrasies'.

Ultimately, the Autobahn was only used on the offensive by the Allied tanks, in the last stages of the battle—in the West by the British and Americans, and in the East by the Red Army, advancing rapidly towards its destination: Berlin. In the process, the tank chains ploughed up the all-too-soft concrete to such an extent that the affected carriageways were still unusable long after the end of the war. When Russian shock troops entered the territory of the German Reich, they could not but marvel at the manicured small towns and the quality of the streets in general. Vasily Grossmann, the Soviet war correspondent, recorded the astonishment of the Red Army fighters: it was incomprehensible to them how inhabitants of such immaculate dwelling places could have set out to invade the uncultivated lands of Russia of all places.

A simple Wehrmacht soldier, travelling on foot at the end of the war, will later note: 'The next morning we reached the motorway from Berlin to Stettin. On the empty road we went north again. The cart rolled better now, and we got back on track. Was this still war at all, this aimless trek through a deserted land?' Thus Dieter Wellershoff in *Der Ernstfall* (The Emergency), the novel recounting his youth in the Third Reich and the final months of the war spent as a volunteer in the Hermann Göring Tank Division. The final chapter is set this side of the River Oder: four soldiers in retreat with a handcart, loaded with weapons and ammunition, while Russian tank units push forward in haste on the Autobahn towards Berlin.

In his life story (*When Memory Comes*), Israeli historian Saul Friedländer captures the moment he steps onto German soil for the first time after the war. It is 1962; he is travelling for research purposes and in Schleswig-Holstein, near the Danish border, he is scheduled to meet a man who was once Commander-in-Chief of the German Navy and, for a few days after Hitler's suicide, as the country lay in ruins, the last head of state of the German Reich: Admiral of the Fleet Dönitz. Friedländer drives north crossing the whole length of vast country and starts to become uneasy on the Autobahn:

> The landscape that passed me to the left and right, yielding completely before my gaze, suddenly began to change its appearance at Mannheim. It was not quite fear nor panic that gripped me but, rather, a strange sense of despair: this motorway would keep me trapped in Germany forever; everywhere Germany, everywhere Germans. I felt as if I had fallen into a trap from which

Schaubild einer Reichsautobahn

there was no escape. The faces passing me in the heavy car suddenly seemed horribly fat and bloated; every single one of the road signs—in German!—was a cold order issued by an almighty, destructive police bureaucracy. . . .

A similar feeling must have affected the Berlin emigrant Gabriele Tergit. On one of her first visits after the war she was travelling with a delegation of journalists and wrote: 'They kept us driving forever. "That's one of the Autobahn motorways!" says an American.'

At this point a poem comes into my mind unbidden, a childhood memory from the post-war time in the shadow of the motorway. Just a few lines capture the incursion of history into the life of a boy. The Polish poet Adam Zagajewski born in Lvov or Lemberg, in 1945 and raised in Gilwice, dreamt like many of his age of making great archaeological discoveries. What he discovered instead was a path back into the violent history of his century. In Lemberg, which had originally been Austrian, later Polish and became part

63

of the Soviet Union after the Hitler–Stalin pact, German troops
had murdered almost half a million people, most of them Jews but
also Poles. After the end of the war the Polish population, including
the Zagajewskis, were resettled and found themselves in Gleiwitz,
in Upper Silesia, now Gilwice, the town where, on 1 September
1939, an orchestrated provocation by agents of Himmler had given
rise to the war.

HIGHWAY

I was maybe twenty.
In the junkyard under the viaduct built
by Hitler I hunted for relics from that war, relics
of the iron age, bayonets and helmets of whichever
army, I didn't care, I dreamed of great discoveries—
just as Heinrich Schliemann once
sought Hector and Achilles in Asia Minor,
but I found neither bayonets
nor gold, only rust was everywhere,
rust's brown hatred; I was afraid
that it might penetrate my heart.

III

THE AERIAL WAR OF IMAGES

Berlin, Charlottenburger Chaussee

Five years after the end of the most murderous war of modern times, Hannah Arendt arrives in Germany on a visit. The philosopher from Königsberg, whose work is currently enjoying a renaissance and is finally being published in a complete edition after the many scattered individual works, returns to her home country for the first time after the catastrophe. 'The Aftermath of Nazi Rule', published later in German under the title 'Ein Besuch nach Deutschland 1950' (A Visit to Germany in 1950), captures in essay form what she saw and thought at the time, an eyewitness account, first published in New York. 'Watching the Germans busily stumbling through the ruins of a thousand years of their own history, shrugging their shoulders at the destroyed landmarks, or resentful when reminded of the deeds of horror that haunt the rest the world, one comes to realize that busyness has become their chief defence against reality.'

When I order the German edition from Rotbuch Verlag, the antiquarian book-delivery service offers me three more titles: Florian Huber, *Child, Promise Me You'll Shoot Yourself: The Downfall of Ordinary Germans in 1945*, Alexandra Senfft, *Silence Hurts: A German Family History*, and Rolf Peter Sieferle, *Finis Germania*— no random selection it seems to me, and with that we are right in middle of the grey zones of the 'memory culture', where every German tries to make sense of their own past. As she travels through southern Germany, Hannah Arendt sees the destroyed cities, gathers impressions and talks to people as any good reporter would. She meets Karl Jaspers and Martin Heidegger, teachers and comrades, but that is not what the report is about. She focuses on the mood of the survivors, the buried inner life of the people who have been bombed out of their homes, who walk through the landscape of ruins like ants. She notes the shadow of deep dejection that hangs over this people, asks about the effects of war, and tries to interpret the nightmare left behind for the rest of the world by a physically, morally and politically ruined Germany. From a contemporary perspective, it seems that only this one observer, Arendt, held on to the wisdom of a modern Pallas Athena. There is a clarity of tone that is absent in the work of her academic colleagues at the time, apart from the representatives of the Frankfurt School who had seen this coming. It is true that Max Horkheimer's *Eclipse of Reason* of 1947 (only published in German twenty years later under the title *Zur Kritik der instrumentellen Vernunft*, The Critique of

Instrumental Reason) and the future theoretical classic *Dialektik der Aufklärung* (Dialectic of the Enlightenment) of 1944 both paved the way; but it was to be a whole generation before their views reached a German audience and became the starting point for a new historical consciousness among future thinkers and poets.

An unmistakable irony and clear-sighted acumen resonate in words of the woman returning home from transatlantic exile. It is this refreshingly austere, optimistic melody that now makes her writing so readable again, the chief witness of the failure of democracy. In her search for truth, she—'cheerfully' in Nietzsche's sense—perceives all kinds of deficits in the essential 'German being'. And the manner of the post-war German nation on its foolish journey had long been familiar to her, as a member of the nation of 'thinkers and poets'. The repressed, the unspoken, even that which could barely be addressed by the deepest minds of the age in the face of recent history, does not escape her. The eternal lack of political clarity: 'What one is up against is not indoctrination, but the incapacity or unwillingness to distinguish altogether between fact and opinion.'

She explores the deeply rooted self-pity of the vanquished, their instinctive flight from reality, the nihilistic relativism that makes them doubt the possibility of any kind of humanity after the total disaster.

Amid the ruins, the Germans write each other picture postcards still showing the cathedrals and marketplaces, public buildings and bridges that no longer exist. And the indifference with which they walk through the rubble finds its exact counterpart in the absence of mourning for the dead; or the apathy with which they react, or rather fail to react, to the fate of the refugees in their midst.

That same year another woman was travelling across Germany in pursuit of the same question: how it can be that the suffering of so many millions of their fellow countrymen, refugees and displaced ethnic Germans now housed in collective accommodation and camps can mean so very little to those in a better situation who have not been bombed out of house and home. Ré Soupault, the wife of the founder of surrealism Philippe Soupault, née Meta Erna Niemeyer from Bublitz in Pomerania, has been commissioned by several Paris newspapers to travel through the defeated nation. Her life up until then has been exemplary of the modern independent woman, with studies at the Bauhaus in Weimar, periods spent as a film assistant, fashion stylist, photographer, member of surrealist circles; now she is in the business of reporting with the utmost objectivity on the camps which house those displaced ethnic Germans, families living in burrows and neglected children who drift through the destroyed country, begging and stealing. Like Arendt, her research comes up time and again against the German repression of recent history.

A conversation about the causes is scarcely possible; very few have had any spare time for reflection. The defeat crashed over them like a shockwave; they had all been fed false information by the regime until the very end. So deeply were ordinary Germans implicated in Hitler's politics of victory that complete amnesia was all that could help them now. That also explains the curiously sweeping historicization of what had happened only recently, so that it had basically already been relegated to the ancient past. This is the wording of the 'Charter for German Expellees' of 1950:

'We Expellees reject all thought of revenge or retribution. The vow is serious and holy in recognition of the endless pain the last decade has wrought upon humanity.' The last decade is guilty, concludes Ré Soupault, not those particular individuals who have had a decisive influence on the fate of the world in that last decade and beyond. Among those she asks she is met with incomprehension. Only among the refugees is there any mention of those Nazi criminals who instigated this war.

This linguistic reticence is even more the case in respect of literature. The caesura was so complete that even traditional narrative forms lay buried in the rubble. In the years after the so-called 'Year Zero' there was for a long time no book that could find words for the collapse. Those who had survived, authors as well as journalists, began the difficult search for a language for a new beginning. Gabriele Tergit, the best-known court reporter of the Weimar era, a German writer of Jewish origins who later emigrated to the UK, author of the successful novel *Käsebier erobert den Kurfürstendamm* (1932), published in English as *Käsebier Takes Berlin*, returns in 1948 to a devastated Berlin and, on meeting publisher Peter Suhrkamp, notes: 'And now fifteen years after an epoch overflowing with talent, Peter Suhrkamp tells me: "We have no new manuscripts. We had expected all the drawers to be full to bursting with stories novels and above all dramas."'

Hannah Arendt's findings anticipate much that still troubles us today. Once again, a huge wave of migration is underway, wars create thousands of displaced people and refugees; and those from poor regions in Africa and Asia set out in search of the paradises of the better off. Once again, those fortunate and successful in

Germany cut themselves off from the rest and determine the course of German politics with their fear of loss. A nationalist egotism is abroad in which democracy, media pluralism and diversity of opinion are being badmouthed as they were at the end of the Weimar Republic.

One of the first to attack this fatalism in a Republic without Republicans was Heinrich Mann in his essay collection *Der Hass* (Hatred), which appeared in the late summer of 1933 in the Amsterdam publishing house Querido, when the author was already in exile, with a dedication 'To My Fatherland'. There he says a good deal about the problem of German nationalism that always seems to grow in strength when attempts to mediate between different nations and indeed within a single nation fail. As an attempt to revise the seemingly inevitable, this volume should find its proper place among today's history books.

There are phrases that resonate to this day in the context of German history. 'Even if it was only a relative freedom, it was still the freest system of government that Germany has ever known', he declares in a positive turn against the spirit of the time. 'The people were set on a good path; they were only stopped by their economic hardship.'

His analysis of the situation of Germany at the end of the Weimar Republic is marked by unparalleled clarity: 'When the forces of reaction and the idea of the nation had become conjoined in people's minds, National Socialism could finally erupt, the great new movement, the movement of stagnation, the novelty of a phenomenon of old age, the demand of the crippled and empty for movement and impetus.' In this Heinrich Mann dared to say openly something that Karl Kraus, the most eloquent critic of his time, could not permit himself to say, so as not to endanger the readers of his journal *Die Fackel*, when he claimed: 'When I think of Hitler, nothing comes to mind.'

But plenty of things came immediately to Henrich Mann's mind and he found only clear words for the situation: his diagnosis of the end of the Weimar Republic. Clearly, he was someone who could peer into a crystal ball. With astonishing foresight, he felt his way towards a vision encompassing everything that is to be found in today's history books: 'A re-armed Germany would be sent forward against Soviet Russia, which would be alone in the sense of the old system. In all probability, the system would be defeated; one does not defeat a revolution whose idea is supported by the given reality and has like-minded people on the opposite side.' And exactly this came to pass, albeit not until twelve years later, agonizingly long, hopeless years in which millions of Jews were murdered, millions of soldiers bled to death on the battlefields, and entire cities from Europe to Japan sank into dust and rubble.

By the time Hannah Arendt visited the results of Nazi fury, what someone like Heinrich Mann, relying on his humanism, foresaw as early as 1933, had also become apparent to the rest of the world: 'Nationalism is finally deadlocked, both politically and economically, it no longer secures a state, and it destroys people. [...] Unbiased thinking is finished in a closed nation-state.' Something to hold on to; it has not lost any of its validity to this day.

Heinrich Mann, by no means a Marxist, but an honest republican and a European spirit, wrote sentences like this as the darkness fell around him: 'Moreover, the Treaty of Versailles has just been signed; this was necessarily a product of the same nationalism that once made the people ripe for war'. The acknowledgement of the supranational was generally considered to be betrayal, and not only in Germany; the pacificism of the war-weary was demonized. The fear that European nations could stumble into another war was dismissed as indulgence on the part of a small group of cosmopolitans.

Heinrich Mann saw things more clearly than most of his contemporaries; but his more famous brother also became a staunch defender of the fragile Republic in the late 1920s. In the face of attacks from the right-wing press, he held firm to the idea of reconciliation among neighbouring countries and engaged himself for European understanding. Shortly after his expatriation, he recognized National Socialism for what it was, a 'degenerate democracy'. So, this was what a morally defunct socialism looked like, populism as a form of mastery, based on a world view that could count on the support of the ignorant and uncultivated, as he claimed in 1938 in a speech given in fifteen American cities: 'On the Future Victory of Democracy'.

On her tour of the German ruins, Hannah Arendt notices the defeated nation's strange lack of empathy with its own fate. The 'inability to mourn' had already struck her as a symptom, years before the psychologists Alexander and Margarete Mitscherlich made the well-known diagnosis of Germany. 'In France and Great Britain, people feel a greater sadness about the relatively few landmarks destroyed in the war than the Germans do for all their lost treasures together.' Arendt, the political thinker, is puzzled by the immediate anti-democratic reflex of so many of her defeated German countrymen, a stance not even softened by the recent experiences during the Hitler dictatorship. 'The average German seeks the causes of the last war not in the acts of the Nazi regime, but in the events that led to the expulsion of Adam and Eve from Paradise.' Not a stone remained standing, but among the displaced and the uprooted, those who had been bombed out of their homes, the result was above all pure self-pity and a kind of hardened numbness in the face of the ruined cities and the personal losses of each individual. All they had left was a malicious joy in ruination— 'a carefully cultivated Schadenfreude'.

What should the world community make of this tribe, who took up their everyday lives on the heels of the currency reform and began to rebuild on every side? A people like no other on earth, obsessed with work, clearing aside the rubble without a thought and refusing to grasp how it could have come to this. This is how the world sees Germany; even if Germany, with its motorways and steel mills, its chemical plants and mechanical-engineering factories, with all the economic achievements of its ant-like diligence, has never been able to see itself in this light.

And it was these key industries and buildings of strategic military importance that had been the targets of the Allied bombers before the so-called 'morale bombing', still disputed by many today, finally became an official war policy. But despite the devastating bombing raids on railway lines, steel mills and fuel refineries, it is precisely these industries that rose phoenix-like from the ashes. The paralysis of the entire system of production feared by the Minister for Armament Albert Speer had, in any case, failed to materialize, while entire cities of cultural significance, along with their historical centres were razed to the ground. Neither the staying power of the troops, nor the endless forbearance of the civilian population could be broken in this way. Even the centres of the arms industry were

only ever destroyed in part. Just days after the firestorm, trains returned to the front through the completely flattened city of Dresden, traffic poured over the Elbe bridges, and armament production continued almost unabated in Saxony, *the weaponsmith of the Reich.*

What was incomprehensible to the world at large, however, was the silence of most Germans after their crashing defeat in May 1945, a case of almost clinical mutism, an expression of a previously unknown social shock phobia, one pervading an entire people.

Later, a whole new field of research would open up based on these ideas: 'psychohistory', pioneered by a thinker like Robert Jay Lifton, Air Force psychiatrist in Japan and Korea, and his investigations into the causes and consequences of wars and political violence. *The Broken Connection: On Death and the Continuity of Life* and *The Genocidal Mentality: Nazi Holocaust and Nuclear Threat* were the milestones of his research, shaped by early psychological studies of Adolf Hitler and by Sigmund Freud's ideas on the effects of collective libidinal delusion. The theory of brainwashing provided him with the key to understanding the psychological manipulation of large sections of the population using isolation, scenarios of threat (street terror, concentration camps, deportation) and sealing individuals off from others who allegedly constitute a threat and must be resisted. Whether action preceded language or vice versa, one was caught in a vicious circle from the beginning of the Hitler regime. Propaganda did the rest along with the mechanisms of intimidation within the dictatorship itself, until everyone found their language brought into line to such an extent that they could no longer think of any alternative, no longer knew what to do with their own thoughts. The present had closed over the life of the individual like the slab of a tomb.

The mendacious language of National Socialism, a prime example of the poisoning of language through deadening rhetoric, had in the end created a collective speechlessness that led to elementary forms of language withering away. It is here that that the mystery of Fascism lies buried to this day. After the bitter end, a cloak of silence was laid over everything. For those of us born afterwards, accustomed to the pretty much permanent discussion of these twelve tragic years of history, this speechlessness seems remarkable. Despite all the attempts by experts to come to terms with it, it is still difficult to get to the bottom of this fact. There are history books, there were the annual German Historians' conventions and the 'historians quarrel' of the late 1980s, and then there is the murky field of popular opinion, with its visions and revisions. This much is clear: Germany was split in two after the Hitler war.

At their Tehran and Yalta conferences the Allies had decided to split the German bearskin. A red line on the map: and families, life stories, narratives were divided forever. The result was not only a geographical and political division but also the divided consciousness of a whole nation—the pathological German–German schism, a kind of schizophrenia (comparable only to that of South and North Korea) that is still in existence. From that moment on, Germans were silent in two languages. And even today, the Germans are surprised when the crust breaks open, repressed memories belch out as if from a clogged drain producing new parties and conflicts (Red Army Faction, National Socialist Underground, Pegida, the recent murders)—and everything starts all over again, apparently beyond comprehension or moderation.

In the East where I was born (in the ruins of Dresden), the straw men in Moscow's pay, officials of the NKVD or People's Commissariat for Internal Affairs such as Walter Ulbricht, who had survived Stalin's persecution of the Communist International, the terror of purges and the nightly arrests of like-minded people in the hotel Lux, built the GDR state. Historian Andreas Peterson gives a powerful account in his *The Men from Moscow: How the Trauma of Stalinism Defined the GDR*. In the West, Adenauer had arrived on the scene and mobilized his Christian Democrats; the doughty mayor of Cologne, side-lined by the Nazis, a Rhinelander for whom the River Elbe was a border beyond which the horrors of Asia began.

I was born into this state of affairs; someone who is still to this day trying to develop the whole film and gain a historical overview of this landscape of destruction.

The writer W. G. Sebald made the complex of this uncanny collective silence the subject of a series of lectures (held at Zurich University in 1997): *Luftkrieg und Literatur* (published in English as *On the Natural History of Destruction*). On the one hand, it responds to the enormous achievement of post-war reconstruction, carried out in grim silence, with the interesting observation that a necessary precondition was certainly 'the unquestioning work ethic learned in a totalitarian society, the capacity for logistical improvisation shown by an economy under constant threat [. . .] and the lifting of the heavy burden of history that went up in flames between 1942 and 1945 along with the centuries-old buildings accommodating homes and businesses in Nuremberg and Cologne, in Frankfurt, Aachen, Brunswick and Würzburg, a historical burden ultimately regretted by only a few.' The virtues so often praised as archetypically German—the work ethos, the thoroughness, the readiness to make sacrifices, the enormous craftsmanship—were in fact behaviours repeatedly activated by the inhabitants of this territory in historical situations of crisis. In the Third Reich these were exacerbated by the compulsion to self-sufficiency and the war-related economy of scarcity. The German ability to perform at its best, even with all sorts of substitute materials and a life dependent on food stamps and emergency rations. The erratic silence of most Germans thus proved to be the flip side of the will to persevere right until the last moment, something incomprehensible to neighbouring countries.

Sebald understands the signs of such social hardening and linguistic devastation and the noticeable emotional vacuum of the post-war years as a result of the obedience internalized during the years of the reign of terror.

Twelve years of being whipped into shape and subjected to an authoritarian education had taught the Germans not to ask questions. Looking back, hardly any of the survivors of the massive city bombardments get beyond a few stunned phrases. Rarely can they produce an unsparing and objective account of what they witnessed. As with death notices, these accounts are always peppered with standard metaphors, tried and tested formulae, conventional language as practised in Goebbels' media empire.

The reality of total destruction, incomprehensible in its extreme contingency, pales when described in such stereotypical phrases as 'prey to the flames', 'that fatal night', 'everything was ablaze', 'all hell was let loose', 'we were staring into the inferno', 'the dreadful fate of the cities of Germany' and the like. Their function is to cover up and neutralize experiences beyond our capacity to comprehend.

But the critic of such stereotypical phrases does not shy away from scrutinising those eyewitness accounts until now considered beyond reproach. For example, Victor Klemperer, dedicated critic of language, author of the *LTI*, a chronicle of the crisis of language in the Third Reich, principal witness of the state crimes against his Jewish fellow citizens in his Saxon hometown, must suffer the indignity of having his own diary entry about the end of Dresden taken to task for remaining within the bounds of verbal convention. 'From what we now know about the ruin of this city it seems unlikely that anyone who stood on the Brühl Terrace with the air full of flying sparks, and saw the panorama of the burning city can have escaped with an unclouded mind.'

But why not? Klemperer—and his account bears witness to this on every page—did not stand there with an unbroken heart when the city perished around him, but in all probability with an unclouded mind. His distanced description of the disastrous night certainly had nothing to do with repression and resistance to trauma. Indeed, Klemperer, born in Landsberg an der Warthe, where the poet Gottfried Benn led his famous 'double life' as a military doctor, was one of the greatest admirers of the city. His diary is, beyond all the adversities of everyday life under Fascism, a declaration of love for Dresden—the city and its culture: Dresden, where he struggled to survive on a daily basis, long before its demise, and whose involuntary chronicler he now became.

On the day the bombers came, he was out on the street doing his job as a postman and delivering deportation orders on behalf of the Gestapo. Among them one to a young mother and her four-year-old child. The terrible episode has imprinted itself on me because it was, as it were, a prelude to the great moment of salvation when Dresden's Jews experienced the firestorm (if, of course, like Klemperer, they did survive). It was a happy coincidence that a direct hit set fire to the Gestapo headquarters in the former Columbia hotel, behind the main railway station, and that in the random lottery of this bombing campaign the local *Judenkartei*, the index listing local Jews, burnt along with it.

No one knows what became of the young mother and her child (an official form had named Auschwitz as the ultimate destination for the pair of them), but the next day henchmen from the bombed-out headquarters had already started hunting for the Jewish runaways. It is quite possible that the relief with which the Jews of Dresden (including the postman Klemperer) accepted the demise of their city without illusion or emotion, led to a rationalization of the horrors. Those condemned to death cannot afford tears, and if so, only at a safe distance—that of exile (in Israel, America or elsewhere). Klemperer's unlikely escape in the last days of the war allowed him, the survivor, who reported on it all, no chance to wallow in his own feelings of pain, in the extravagant manner of Marcel Proust for example, whom he so admired.

The weeks after the downfall of Dresden became yet another fight for survival for Klemperer and his wife Eva, demanding all their strength and leaving no time for mourning. To claim that the apocalyptic events have been depicted on a randomly fixed canvas, and only within the bounds of conventional language, misses the mark at least in this case.

It is true that Klemperer remains remarkably composed when describing the night of devastation, but for reasons that are perfectly comprehensible. Like others, he also focuses on apparently circumstantial details; and he certainly never veers into the visionary, like Erich Nossack in his account of the destruction of Hamburg, *Der Untergang* (*The End*). In that novel the incomprehensible aspect at the heart of the catastrophe shifts, at the very climax, into a dream sequence foretelling the end of the world. At this point the narrative itself begins to stutter. 'To forget! A few of those who remained lay the on the naked round of the world [...]. Then someone began to talk in his sleep. No one understood what he was saying. [...] "I confess: we were human!"'

Apart from this, Sebald's remarks on aerial war are nowhere unclear or in any way circumscribed in their perspective. Sebald called Alexander Kluge, author of the only radically analytical study of aerial war on his hometown, *Air Raid on Halberstadt on 8 April 1945*, the most enlightened of all (German) writers and notes: 'The ironic amazement with which he registers the facts allows him to maintain the distance of an observer—indispensable for any kind of discovery'. The truth is that Sebald himself is certainly the most empathetic observer in modern German. At the very least, he is considered to be the ultimate instance to date of a comprehensive moral perspective on the catastrophic events—including the perspective of Jews, Germans and those involved in the War on the side of the Allies, especially the British Air Force.

The author of *Austerlitz* and *The Rings of Saturn* is still the only bridgehead allowing German readers, bound to their own narrative of history, to grasp some of the commonality in loss. None other than the professor of Modern German Literature at the University of East Anglia in Norwich could have written phrases like this: 'But I do not necessarily have to return to Germany and my place of origin, to visualize that period of destruction. It often comes back to my mind where I live at present. Many of the more than seventy airfields from which the war of annihilation was waged against Germany were located in the county of Norfolk.'

Thus, it is necessary to head deep into foreign territory, behind the former fronts, to find a vantage point from which to reflect with this degree of clarity as a German author. When I started reading Sebald's books, I had no picture of the author in my mind. Though in his memorable travel narrative, with its search for traces in Vienna, Verona, Venice and Riva, the bit that remained with me especially was the depiction of the return home to a small Alpine resort, in the chapter 'Ritorno in patria', which it only later struck me was the biographical core of his narrative project.

What good fortune, I think today, that we met once after all, though by chance. Both of us were caught up in the whirlwind of literary business, that picked up speed in the late 90s, and gradually drove the competing authors at book fairs, publishing houses and all other public performance venues into solitude. Yet out of it came the moment I still draw on today. Such chance encounters are rarely given in a poet's life. Berlin-Tegel, flight to Frankfurt, I had just buckled myself into one of the back seats, when a man makes his way towards me from the front and leans over: Sebald is his name, he says he already knows who I am. He had read my first volumes of poetry and was glad to finally meet me in the flesh. He had a copy of the Berlin *Tagesspiegel* tucked under his arm. There he was: the much-discussed author who lived in England shrouded in secrets. I had only read one of his books at that point, *Schwindel Gefühle* (*Vertigo*) which, however, I had read back to front twice over, recognizing an extraordinary prose work. And now he had come over to me, in literary terms a stowaway on this flight, to look me direct in the eye—a scene I tried to develop many times because, after his premature death in an accident the following year, it appeared more and more to me like one of those unlikely events, coincidences in time and space, that can shape a writer's life. 'Such are the abysses of history. Everything in them lies in confusion, and when you look down into them, you are seized with horror and vertigo.'

As if that was what he intended, I have often thought of him since: the traveller, the time-traveller with his high forehead, the sad eyes behind large spectacles and the beard of a seal, who immediately instilled confidence in me because he reminded me of a Saxon philosopher with whose writings I grew up: Friedrich Nietzsche. As I said, this encounter preceded knowledge of his amazing work, and perhaps for that reason it continues to resonate within me to this day.

One day—I was in London once again, a festival at one of the new cultural palaces on the south bank of the Thames had invited the poets of the world to come together—history was to catch up with me once more. It was around this time that I had begun to observe my life from outside as diarists do. For the first time it was making itself felt at least in broad outline as it does to this day. I, the East German, one of those scattered across the globe after the fall of the Berlin Wall, was running around the streets of the city like 'counterfeit money' (or what the English would call a spare prick at a wedding). The counterfeit money was the euro, which only a few years before had been introduced as the new currency in the western part of the continent.

Where Piccadilly meets Hyde Park Corner, I ran into a crowd of people, a memorial was being unveiled—an event that in the next moment I realized affected me. After the RAF monument on the bank of the Thames and a statue of Bomber Harris on the Strand, it had finally been decided to honour the British bomber pilots of the Second World War with a monument of their own (The Bomber Command Memorial), and just as I came wandering past was the moment that it was solemnly being made public. Out there in the world I felt, not for the first time, like the little Dresden boy from Erich Kästner's memoir. It was one of those eyewitness moments that remain with you—as someone touched personally by the history they entail.

I remember that the ceremony had just ended, Her Majesty Queen Elizabeth II had already left, and I, a German spy, went over to the ranks of the RAF veterans. Old men, many of them in wheelchairs, with a huge familial apparatus in tow attending to the grey gentlemen, sympathetic fellows all of them, grouped around

their heroes, soldiers of the bombing war against the German cities. I saw grandfathers, highly decorated men, and saw the monument, freshly unveiled, a group of brown giants in bronze, strange creatures emerging from the mud of history in their official attire. They were set up in a kind of shrine, reliefs of different models of bomber plane on the walls, a crew of seven in a painfully realistic style, correct down to the last detail of the uniforms, with a radio and leather caps. The sculpture would not have stood up to critical scrutiny for even a second, but none of those gathered there seemed bothered by that. One had to admit: the culture of remembrance had gone its own way, not adhering to the avant-garde rules of art, a crude realism was all it needed. Those in attendance smiled for the cameras and were in an almost light-hearted mood on this bright June day, friendly even to the stranger in their midst. He did not belong there, but times had changed, everyone was welcome—all forgiven, if not quite forgotten. About a third of the air crews had been killed during the bombing sorties: in total 55,000 RAF men. Why should the descendants not put up their own kind of memorial to them, one that didn't give a damn about the niceties of modern sculpture?

I can still remember the approach to London by air, which I experienced in a rare euphoria at the time, on account of the glorious summer weather. The sense of promise began at the mouth of the Thames estuary. The view had been so extraordinary, the panorama of the capital so razor sharp on the horizon that I was involuntarily put in mind of the pilots and on-board gunners of the Royal Air Force in the glass cockpits of the Vickers Wellington and Avro Lancaster aircraft. As cool as you like, I saw the great European city appear like a target spread before me. Dreamily, I had followed the Thames as it meandered towards the high-rise towers in the distance, saw the Millennium Dome, a white hedgehog, Canary Wharf and the Docklands, and recognized in the majestic course of the river, as in a film dissolve, the famous S-shape of the River Elbe at my hometown Dresden. Not only the rivers, also our cities bound together by war, suddenly opened up before me in all their beauty and defencelessness from this perspective of a bird of prey, and I was, I remember, moved in an inexplicable way.

There it was again, the war of aerial photographs. Not for the first time it occurred to me that the destruction of the landscape, human conurbations and the industrial areas vital for war on the ground, had been preceded by their mapping from the air, impressive survey images created with the aid of photography. Only the precise aerial images, the capturing of enemy sites in a grid of squares, had made possible the preparations of the bomber strategists. And ironically enough, it had been postcards, tourist images, so-called aerial views, that had provided the template. Not only

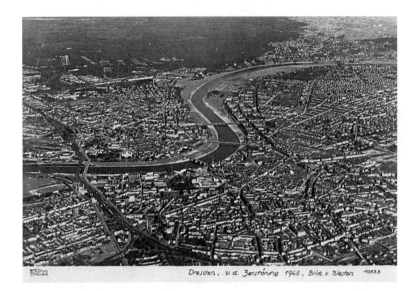

Dresden, u. d. Zerstörung 1945, Blick v. Westen 10533

had tourist destinations like Dresden, treasures of world culture been proudly pictured, but also entire industrial zones with every detail of blast furnaces, refineries, harbours and production plants. For example, an aerial image of excellent quality produced by Baden Pfalz Lufthansa shows the 'Neckarspitze' at Mannheim, the place where the Rhine and the Neckar converge. The mandatory notice 'reproduction prohibited' only concerned the copyright for the image itself, not its potential use in aerial reconnaissance by enemy forces.

Printed in large editions at a time when photography became the new medium of precision, such overviews of the terrain were also available to future enemies, providing orientation for the aerial reconnaissance teams with their new large-screen cameras.

In the total war soon to come, air-force strategists discovered their targets had already been comprehensively documented. On

Flugzeugaufnahme von Mannheim-Neckarspitze

the light tables in the command centres lay photographs taken by reconnaissance fliers, single images in high resolution, on which every road, and every settlement could be clearly identified—including the Jewish ghettos in the east of the continent and even the barracks of Auschwitz, that place of terror, the function of which was shrouded in uncertainty, although the report by the Polish underground spy, Jan Karski, that had been personally presented to President Roosevelt at a private audience, left no doubt about the function of gas chambers and crematoria. One of the many uncanny facets of the Second World War is the way the eye of the camera intruded into every aspect of life, allowing photography to be instrumentalized as a weapon, and not least the fact that each army was well informed about the other in terms of image technology long before the deployments began.

The German cities, seen from above, from a defenceless perspective—long before Google Maps—this was an involuntary act of self-disclosure that the enemy could easily exploit. In the case of Dresden, for example, there was the photographer Walter Hahn, the Studio Hahn with his own selection of printed post cards. Thousands of the most beautiful postcard images of Dresden and the surroundings can be traced back to this one bustling entrepreneur. In the 1920s he had already shifted his business interests to views of the famous baroque city, he was the man of the hour in the period of emerging city tourism. His recipe for success: to take photographs only in good weather and with beautiful cloud formations.

He had begun his work with images of mountains: clouds above the cliffs of Saxon Switzerland. Like his predecessors, the painters of Romanticism, he had first been inspired by the picturesque natural surroundings, but he turned to the city, favoured by its location in the Elbe Valley, to form a natural overall picture. In his images Dresden truly appears like 'that pearl on the Elbe' which, according to Adolf Hitler, only National Socialism could promise to give its proper setting. Looking at Walter Hahn's images you can see how the city appears as part of the natural history of this region, so successfully had he choreographed the images to create that story. A typical businessman of his day, he became a Nazi Party member in 1934; only shortly after the end of the war, freshly de-Nazified, he was already receiving his first new commissions—someone like him would always be needed. The Third Reich passed him by like a sniffle from which he soon recovered.

His entrepreneurial calculations had panned out magnificently. During the twelve years of Nazi rule, he was the only one allowed

to take aerial photographs in the region of Saxony, with a special permit from the Propaganda Ministry. The advertising aviator Ernst Fröde went for jaunts with him in the search for the best images. He is also alleged to have flown with Ernst Udet, one of the aviation legends of the First World War, whom Hermann Göring, Reich Aviation Minister and himself a Second World War pilot, courted as a folk hero. Udet was the inventor of the 'Jericho trumpet', an appalling wailing siren used by the Junker Ju 87 dive bombers, popularly called Stukas, to spread fear and terror during their steep descent.

Among the technical innovations ushered in by the military, as the air war had hit its stride and London was experiencing attacks day and night during the Blitz and the unpredictable arrival of the V1 rockets (popularly called doodlebugs), there was also a particular contribution from Dresden: the so-called *Klotzsche-Tisch*. At an air force barracks in the north of the city, troops in the news

service had developed a light table that projected signals from radar onto a tabletop, providing officers on the ground with a precise view of the situation in the air. Serial production began in May 1943. The first devices of this kind were set up in Caen in France, and later delivered to the air defence positions in Paris and Rouen. Did the air war strategists have any idea that their dream of mastering technology would one day literally dissolve into thin air?

The aerial image is the phantasm of false sovereignty. Like the fire-brigade shows staged in the 1930s, the expansion of air-raid shelters and the constant air-raid exercises, it functioned only to bring the bomber squadrons to the fore in the logic of war. An example like the civilian Walter Hahn reveals how the images the Third Reich produced of itself continued to have an effect right up to its downfall. Ordinary everyday life in the different quarters of the city and on the streets only appears at the margins in his work. People with their daily pursuits and needs intrude into the picture only by chance; they are in truth undesirable disturbances in a sublime Veduta aesthetic that only celebrates landmarks, famous works of architecture under the ever-radiant skies. Only at the very end can they be seen, in burning clumps, piled up amidst the smoking rubble, heaps of corpses. This was the last assignment: Hahn documents the humanitarian catastrophe, the corpses being take away in carts, bodies burning on metal grilles in Dresden's Altmarkt Square. So it is that people inevitably begin to appear in the pictures: representatives of the Technical Relief Agency employed in an emergency capacity, including, it is said, special forces from extermination camps to the east, men who had learnt their trade in Treblinka and Sobibor.

The air war unleashed by the Germans themselves—in Guernica, Warsaw, Coventry, Rotterdam—had finally come home to roost. The corpses, the rats, the flies, the parasitic fauna of destruction, the whole landscape of decay and rot—the consequences of the war they instigated—and which the Germans,

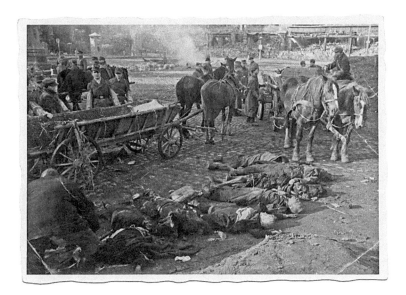

accustomed to order, and with the declared aim of cleansing Europe of all human 'vermin', could never have dreamt of in their administrative areas and well-ordered cities. Erich Nossack's account of the destruction of Hamburg also notes, among other things, the sudden craving for perfume.

The total chaos that eventually rolled over them, the death and debris, the bombed cities turned to wastelands that ushered in the end of their arrogance—this was what could no longer be talked about. At the end of Alexander Kluge's account of the demise of his hometown, Halberstadt, it mentions an American psychologist conducting surveys among German survivors for a study by the Historical Research Centre, Maxwell Airforce Base, Alabama in May 1945: 'It seemed to him as if the population, despite an inborn pleasure in telling stories had, precisely within the contours of the destroyed areas of the town, lost the psychic strength to remember.'

At the ground zero of all annihilation, the extinction of all civilization—this is where a natural history of destruction had to start, if enlightenment were to succeed in the future. And history lessons had to begin right there, not with any other dates from human history. Education by dint of understanding the causes of the disasters that shaped our lives (long before we were born) was the only constructive possibility.

It was necessary to change the Germans' own narrative about themselves and their seemingly so inevitable and disastrous history, to break the spell of collective fatalism by showing them alternatives, so as to heal them of their ridiculous fantasies of superiority, the arrogance of their own making, as Kluge suggested with his 'strategy from below'. In the episode about the primary school teacher Gerda Baethe, the solution is hinted at once, in a casual digression. In the historic subjunctive form, it says that preventing the downfall would have required

> seventy thousand determined schoolteachers, all like herself, each of them teaching hard for twenty years from 1918 onwards in every country involved in the First World War; but also at the national level, pressure on press, on government; then the young people educated in this way, would have been able to seize the reins . . . . It's all a question of organization.

We also encounter the same thought elsewhere, the idea of a positive intervention in the course of history: for example, in the secret diaries of the Stuttgart Democrat and pacifist Anna Haag. She was the rare case of a feminist in the Third Reich, one of the most radical observers of the criminal Nazi state. In her chronicle, Haag, later to become an educational reformer, employs a similar approach in her entry for 6 November 1941, when the turning point of Stalingrad was already on the horizon and the news of the mass murder of the Jews and the Soviet prisoners of war was beginning to reach many German households: 'I certainly, certainly want to do my bit! What mountains of work! But everything must be changed from the bottom up: the narrative, at home and in school and college above all else'.

Anna Haag's diary, even now accessible only in excerpts in Germany and brought to light, not by chance by a British researcher, the cultural historian Edward Timms, is a treasure trove of the first order. It is one of the few examples of a political reappraisal of the everyday life of the Germans in dark times. Haag is pained by the sophisticated and mendacious propaganda of Nazism. The words she keeps coming back to are always: barbarism and mendacity, the oppressive apparatus of the Gestapo and SS, the false sense of community and the bovine faith of those poisoned by the leadership. She sees through the perfidious propaganda system of blackmail, the indoctrination into hatred, the remote control of all, a policy of stoking fear that led everyone to distrust everyone else and neighbours to denounce each other without a second thought. But afterwards no one could admit that it had been them, no one could admit that they knew anything about the great crimes and the many small ones of their own. On 14 November 1938, she notes: 'Discussions are being held on the final solution of the Jewish question. [. . .] Where will that lead?' And when she receives a letter from a frontline soldier from her circle of acquaintances (22 May 1943): 'How, she asks, could a young man from a devout and cultured Christian family come to "believe in a leader who orders him to liquidate Jews, Poles, Russians?"' Where else in private records from this period can you find phrases like this, from which you can clearly deduce what information was common knowledge at the time? She describes the whole circus of her fellow human beings, draws character portraits of those fellow countrymen who would later be sorted by the victorious Allies in categories such as: Major Offender, Offender, Lesser Offender, Follower and Exonerated.

In her diaries, which she, with a teacher's instinct, camouflages as school exercise books and keeps hidden in the coal cellar, she risks her life by keeping a daily record of what happens to her, jotting down anecdotes, often verbatim. The situation is hopeless and the population firmly in the grip of the Nazi administration. What

can individual resistance do in such a state? The height of her sense of powerlessness is caught in her question, a feminist joke: 'CAN YOU KILL HITLER WITH A COOKING SPOON?' (14 May 1942).

In the grotesque image of the cooking spoon lashing out against an almighty dictator lies the total despair of a woman caught in a militaristic society dominated by men's federations, and fixated on revenge and conquest. No wonder it is women who are the first to recognize aggressive nationalism as the root of the evil, children trained as cannon fodder, the bane of conscription, the reproductive politics, the whole doctrine of this state deliberately geared to collective complicity. A woman who heartily abhors patriotism because the soldierly virtues seem to her to be the greatest danger to family life. 'No, I don't want to be "German" any more!' she writes. 'Dear people of England! I implore you to bring a salutary punishment down upon our nation, so this vile arrogance can finally be driven out and we can learn the word *humility* once more! Things are so dire that we cry out for God!'

Early on she saw the air war coming, long before it reached the German cities. The bombing raids on Warsaw, Rotterdam and English cities strike at the very heart of this innate European—her daughter Sigrid lives in Britain, married to an Englishman.

Every day she listens to the BBC news with her husband Albert, a maths teacher, in their remote house on the edge of the forest in a suburb of Stuttgart ('Broadcasting Crimes' was the official term, 'Impairment of Defence', for which, if discovered, they could be sentenced to imprisonment or even death). Charles Richardson and Richard Crossman, familiar broadcasting voices, inform them of the state of the war via the enemy broadcaster. She quotes Churchill and Anthony Eden, learns of the slaughter of Jews in the east, which she immediately understands is a mark of shame, a blemish of biblical proportions. She notes the back and forth of opinions among the disoriented people around her (the pharmacist, the teacher, the farmer), cuts out newspaper articles and sticks them into her diary, quite the amateur historian. From the very beginning, she devotes herself to the question that even now continues to occupy historians: what could the Germans have known? Were they aware of what was happening in the name of Germany?

At the same time, a woman on the other side of the Channel records her 'Thoughts on Peace in an Air Raid' at a symposium on current women's issues, August 1940. In her cottage in Rodmell, Sussex, on the south coast of England, Virginia Woolf cowers beneath the roar of the nightly German bombers flying from Belgium over East Sussex towards London, noting: 'Arms are not given to Englishwomen (sic?) either to fight the enemy or to

defend herself. She must lie weaponless tonight.' She, too, experiences the powerlessness of women during these hours and tells herself: 'If we were free, we should be out in the open, dancing, at the play, or sitting at the window talking together. What is it that prevents us? "Hitler!" the loudspeakers cry with one voice. Who is Hitler? What is he? Aggressiveness, tyranny, the insane love of power made manifest, they reply. Destroy that, and you will be free.' But: 'Women have not a word to say in politics.' Less than four weeks later, her home in Mecklenburg Square, home of the Hogarth Press, is badly damaged by a direct hit. More than a thousand British civilians are killed in this year alone. 'Start of major offensive against England. 2,000 planes set off this morning', notes Goebbels, the official government diarist, cheerfully on 14 August and, quite the master of fake news, immediately falsifies the figures: 'afternoon at 5 p.m. again a major attack on southern England with

4,000 planes.' What the Germans never wanted to know: more than 40,000 people were killed in the air raids on Britain; 100,000 London houses were destroyed in 1944, a further 800,000 were damaged—all this preceded the bombing war against German cities carried out with utmost stringency. The Battle of Britain began with targeted attacks on London, Birmingham, Coventry. On a moonlit night in November 1940, the entire city centre of Coventry was razed to the ground with 500 tonnes of high-explosive bombs and 30,000 firebombs. 'London is burning'—the BBC reports on 8 September 1940 as the Royal Air Force launched itself into battle against the German bomber squadrons flying in along the Thames.

Out of what followed, out of the miserable end of the aggressors, the question must be answered: what can be learnt from history? The Germans had started the war, says Anna Haag, and the only thing left is the bitter observation: 'One beautiful, gentle city after another sinks into rubble and ash!'

Fear of foreign control (today one would say of globalization), the shock of the Great Depression, as the agents of which the Jews were demonized, for supposedly making free with global finance, fear of 'subordination to the Untermensch' and the 'vermin' undermining everyday life—this is what provoked many Germans and eventually whipped them up into a phobic frenzy. Despite unease about the regime's measures—advancing Wehrmacht soldiers complain about hygiene conditions in Eastern Europe and are disgusted by Jewish ghettos set up by German administrators—fear of paralysis and 'corruption of the racial corpus' was also at the root of the measures taken against the mentally ill and handicapped, killed in the interests of public health.

AUSSTELLUNG »DAS SOWJET-PARADIES«
BERLIN, LUSTGARTEN, 9. MAI BIS 21. JUNI 1942

AUSSTELLUNG »DAS SOWJET-PARADIES«
BERLIN, LUSTGARTEN, 9. MAI BIS 21. JUNI 1942

Fear of modernity in general; and in everyday life—fashion, sexuality, art—incomprehension in the face of the dissolution of form in contemporary avant-garde movements. These also provide the background against which the travelling exhibition 'Degenerate Art' created such an impact among the populace (with huge numbers of visitors). Cleansing the temple of art of all modernist aspirations was the stated goal; along with its worship of *Negro sculpture* (Carl Einstein); war on the Expressionist bogeyman, and Judaism in art tout court. But even a propaganda show like *The Soviet Paradise* (put on in Berlin's Lustgarten, May–June 1942)—staged as a perfidious tremolo before the invasion of the Soviet Union, that summarily annulled the Hitler–Stalin pact—could be relied on to build on the German fear of any kind of disorder—with dioramas depicting misery in the Bolshevik state in a series of clichés and provoking horrified reactions among German fellow countrymen.

Even Hitler's suicide in the bunker of the Reich Chancellery, was prompted, rumour has it, by his fear of being dragged through Moscow as a trophy in a rat cage, by the victorious Russians. The fanatical purist feared—literally—being dragged through the dirt. But the invasion of the 'Mongol hordes', the 'Asian' conditions that would await Germany after defeat—where else had they truly been realized than in the extermination camps with their crowds of emaciated victims, the untenable hygienic conditions behind the barbed wire fences? What happened there was unimaginable for the Germans with their obsession with cleanliness. When, after the war, the first pictures emerged of bulldozers shoving piles of naked puppets into pits, the disgust at the sight was the surest basis for repression of what had happened. This is what is supposed to have happened in our name? That cannot be.

Fact and opinion—Hannah Arendt's account of the flight from reality of many Germans and their difficulty facing the truth was the starting point. When a people has caused so much unspeakable horror and then been forced to witness it—cannot it be the case that its mother-tongue closes up, its consciousness shuts down? That is, it lives on, prattles its way through the days to mask the monstrosity of what has happened, but is unable to express its own ideas, articulate a clear thought, assert the historical consistency of its own narrative. For so long the speechlessness had spread among the German people, permeating all areas of life, that when the nightmare was over, they no longer found even the simplest words that could affirm the meaning of living together. Like Lucifer, Nazism had hurled them down into the abyss, and now they, as illiterates, had to start to relearn feeling, thinking, the civilization of a free world—like children.

The war they instigated as voters, tolerated as Fellow Travellers, Hitler's war of aggression, did not seem, when all was said and done, to have been their war. Forced into conscription, they had brought it upon the neighbouring peoples without any clear expectations. They had taken it as far as the Northern Cape, the Volga and Africa. But when it came back to them and devastated their hometowns, they fell silent with fright. In the end they succumbed to the overwhelming, deadening, effects of the events they themselves had set in train, and into the eye of which they stumbled, as into a hurricane. In this silence, in a climate of blindness to one's own guilt, of national misery, I too grew up. And it is no use telling myself that the other German state, the GDR, saw itself as the anti-Fascist bulwark. I know about the deal done between the two roaring dragons (Fascism and Communism), know about the effort to bury the world of western democracy between them. The Hitler–Stalin pact of 1939 will always burn in my memory as a warning.

Whenever someone writes about the ugly years of German aberration, of war and collective blindness, I read it with a certain feeling of tension inside me and am immediately caught up in it again. It shows me that something within me in the mode of historical psychoanalysis is connected to these events, a deeper layer in me is still sensitive to it. All of this may have long since been consigned to history, but it has not really passed. It still penetrates my life with a thousand thorns. It was as if the 'German hysteria' was still jabbering on in my dreams and appealing to my conscience. In fact, the fall of the Wall was the saving grace for me. It was the experience of a total decay of hierarchies: a state had disintegrated, the dictatorship of the Workers' and Peasants' leaders.

Not until this last turn did the German subject—the really existing socialist petty bourgeois, renegade of the great world revolution—die. Only then was Prussia really at an end, the reactive Prussia of the East. If the German Reich had been a Greater Germany under Prussian hegemony from Bismarck to Hitler, the divided Germany was until 1989 a stop gap, a provisional solution to the problem of dismantling the historical legacy and re-educating its populations. On one side, a liberal, market-based democracy tied to the West, and following the example of America; on the other, a socialist state based on a poorly understood Marxist formula, reinforced with barbed wire, supported by the military, and leaning towards the big brother of the Soviet Union until the latter finally cast it adrift.

Born in 1962, I was separated by only seventeen years from the great caesura of 1945—the year that those with a mentality that remains alien to me to this day wished to see declared zero hour. Seventeen years, what is that in historical terms? An adolescence, you might say—or an entire generation. Not only in the sense of the simple sequence of parent and child but also as a position within the historical continuum, although not with the same horizon of experience. That the war shaped successive generations is true. That its aftermath shaped me, from kindergarten on, is something that I try to remain sceptical about—but I become increasingly unsuccessful in that endeavour. If men such as Günter Grass or Dieter Wellershoff belonged to the generation of combatants and young soldiers; and those born around 1929, the so-called *Flakhelfergeneration*, drafted in at the end of the war to man the antitank guns, are known as the 'sceptical generation' with their sharp and nimble minds (Hans Magnus Enzensberger, Kluge,

Habermas, Heiner Müller); and if the so-called white-haired vintages born in the 1930s and early 40s belonged to the 'post-war generation' (like my father, or the German expatriate W. G. Sebald)—where did I belong? I who appeared on the freshly cleared terrain of the 1960s, a year after the building of the Wall that would determine my destiny, until I could, after a further twenty-seven years that seemed like an eternity, head out into the big wide world—the world of today, and still my favourite world?

IV

FOR THE DYING CALVES

The Thousand-Year Reich had come to an end after twelve bloody years.

The 'belated nation', which had drawn the short straw when it came to dividing up the overseas colonies of the world and so colonized inwards with the expulsion of the Jews (GDR writer Heiner Müller's thesis), had become the bogeyman of the world, a disgrace among nations. Germany's dream of expanding eastwards, with military villages and farming communities all the way to the Urals and protectorates everywhere, its evil utopia of world domination, envisaged by its *Führer* Adolf Hitler, was over. So fast that all anyone could do was rub their eyes. Had these Germans lost their minds?

After the war, the previously hyperactive nation with its vision of world domination turned inwards. Now the 'Volk ohne Raum', a nation deprived of its longed-for *Lebensraum*, were to focus instead on the last unspoiled bit of *Heimat* left to them. 'The Fieldpath', extolled by Martin Heidegger, the philosopher of the hour, in his small, but widely read essay of 1953 as vade mecum. Martin Heidegger, forerunner of the eco-movement, secret hero of the Greens? Something abiding had to be found, something tried and tested, unspoilt, something that by its very nature spoke of *Heimat* and made defeat bearable as a kind of renunciation. Because, as the philosopher says: 'The Renunciation does not take. The Renunciation gives. It gives the inexhaustible power of the Simple. The message makes us feel at home in a long Origin.' This was the new programme, an ecological manifesto *avant la lettre*, in a mixture of romanticism and objectivity of the moment, as only a German could write it. There was the lark on a summer's morning, the oak tree on the wayside and the roughly hewn bench, on which 'occasionally there lay [...] some writing or other of the great thinkers, which a young awkwardness attempted to decipher.' And right there was the vision of a world into which those weary of civilization could withdraw from the catastrophe of modernity. Only they, these few, the abiding, will someday be able, through 'the gentle might of the Fieldpath [...], to outlast the gigantic power of atomic energy, which human calculation has artifacted for itself and made into a fetter of its own doing'.

The 'jargon of authenticity' was what another German thinker, Theodor W. Adorno, called it in his critique of ideology based on what he termed linguistic aberrations at odds with modern life—a reckoning with Heidegger's philosophical style. This work was not perhaps the last word on the matter but was nevertheless formative in its polemic. The representatives of the Frankfurt School shelved Heidegger as a problem of linguistic aberration, anti-modern prose. The thinking behind his work was not to be got rid of quite so easily, however; the seminal eco-sound of his philosophy could not be switched off as one switches off the radio. He remained, untouched, beyond competing political programmes, until one day he jumped out at me and plunged me into some confusion.

Zeitgeist or not: the debate read like a commentary on the economic miracle, the time of motorway construction and the booming automobile industry with its Volkswagen, Mercedes and BMWs, *made in Germany*. Who was on whose side? Who cared about the objections of the newly emerging discipline of sociology and Adorno's critique of language set against the logic of origin in the words of the ontologist Heidegger, who had become suspect as a teacher because he had praised the *Führer* in his rector's speech in Freiburg, believing in the platonic discourse of 'tyrannous education'?

The fixation on overcoming the density of populated spaces had, once and for all, been driven out of the little men of the master race who wanted to rule over the peoples of the world, the descendants of the poets and thinkers. Their territory, which on a map of Europe of 1939 after Germany had gained Saarland, annexed Sudetenland and subsequently all of Austria, stretched as far as East Prussia on the border with Lithuania, had now shrunk to the potent core that the victorious powers divided among themselves.

A yeast dough that could no longer rise, that from now on had to be content with what was left of the burnt cake. An area between the North Sea in the West and the River Oder in the East: so little room for such a mighty people. Eighty million people who had to learn their lesson. Several different generations who had to grasp in school, in geography lessons, that this was it, once and for all. No more urge for expansion, justifiable under international law, all outward movement in terms of territory was at an end.

Hitler's last feint had not been credible even for a second: his attempt to present himself as a protector against the oncoming inundation of Bolshevism, the core of his morale-boosting speeches, that *Mein Kampf* was in fact only the expression of a 'final argument about the reorganization of Europe'. The survivors of his adventure were left with only one option, to turn back into a smaller space, to turn inwards, to find diligence and modesty. In this, the Germans were well practised: fantasists, born dreamers, for whom, once they had repressed their national feelings of guilt, only the worship of silence remained. The silence after the final bell tolls. 'It reaches out even to those who were sacrificed before their time through two world wars' (Heidegger). In truth this meant, though, a silence about one's own memory of the dead that tried to pass over the millions of deaths of others in silence too.

A new nation was thus born, a divided one, lifted from the baptismal font by the victorious powers—with the Marshall Plan on the one side and affiliation with the West; on the other side, integration into the Eastern bloc under the control of the Soviet Union—for forty years of decreed division. But after this Cold War limbo between the former Allies who had been involved in a coalition against Hitler, the Germans came together again in a Europe characterized by diverse dissolved power blocks and now needed to discover how it would cope in the epoch of intensified globalization given its precarious position in the middle of the continent.

This is how a speaker at the UN General Assembly in New York could open his speech, a German practised in self-denial. That could be me perhaps. But who am I? Just an observer on the fringe, one of many invited from time to time to speak publicly, about the state of their nation, as here and now in the venerable university town of Oxford (the old city of the oxen-ford at the meeting of the River Cherwell and the Thames), this peaceful university town spared by the bombs and where this slaughter must seem like sheer madness.

What am I trying to say with all this? Quite simply: that history, in capital letters, intruded even into my little life one day. I was still at school, on the outskirts of Dresden, when it first dawned on me what I got myself into, without any of my doing. Beyond the box hedge in front of my childhood home lay an empire that stretched eastwards to the Pacific, to Vladivostok and to Inner Mongolia. Or in the words of Friedrich Hölderlin: 'I am pulled as streams are by the ending of something that stretches away like Asia' (Phaeton Fragments). Hölderlin, another outsider, a poet and misunderstood artist who baffled authority and who served first the nation (and later National Socialism) as a heaven-sent source of quotations because he changed the course of German-language poetry forever.

Two scenes from my childhood are still clear. In the first—a winter's morning in the late seventies—I pull the garden gate behind me and lift my rucksack onto my shoulder. I'm on my way to school when a Russian military convoy made up of Ural-375 troop carriers races past me on Karl-Liebknecht Strasse, and my gaze is caught by the huge, hulking wheels of the vehicles, the felt coats and steel helmets of the soldiers, and I stand stock still in amazement and forget time.

What did I know then of Isaac Babel (*Red Cavalry*), of Mikhail Sholokhov (*And Quiet Flows the Don*), later to be compulsory school reading, or of Vasily Grossmann's *Life and Fate*, a book I read only decades later, once the Soviet Union had long since disappeared? But the image had imprinted itself on me, and from that moment on I began to understand German history from the point of view of the Russians, who were cavorting about here in my hometown, right on the doorstep. In the beginning it was the cartridge cases we boys found in the surrounding woods, military badges, which we bartered with the Russian soldiers at the barracks gates, not two hundred metres from my parents' house, in exchange for photos of naked women (from the only GDR magazine that printed such pictures). And it wasn't until much later that I read Joseph Brodsky, that brilliant Soviet renegade and first poet of the transition from East to West, whose verses immediately struck home: 'In the beginning, there was canned corned beef. More accurately, in the beginning, there was a war. The Second World War; the siege of my hometown, Leningrad; the great hunger, which claimed more lives than all the bombs, shells, and bullets together. And toward the end of the siege, there was canned corned beef from America.'

The second scene is a bit more complicated; we are in the middle of a history lesson in the eighth grade, and the teacher, a strict member of the Party, gives me the task of preparing a lecture, with the theme: the Nuremberg trials. So, I headed to the Saxon State Library, then housed in the city's largest barracks complex, also containing troop accommodations and weapon depots belonging to the Soviet Army and the NVA, or GDR National People's Army. The juxtaposition of scholarship and the military life of the 'fraternal armies', as I experienced it on the way to the silence of the reading room, got me thinking. I procured my first library card and set myself up as a permanent fixture among the books, which soon earned me the respect of the staff and years later led them to allow me to view the archive of Victor Klemperer. At that time hardly anyone outside Dresden knew the author of one of the most important diaries of the Nazi era; he was known only as the author of *LTI*. His private work was only discovered, via the success of the America edition in the West, after the fall of the Berlin Wall. Only then was it recognized across the world for what it is: a rare chronicle of everyday life of the Nazi era in a city (Dresden), from the perspective of an academic dismissed from his post, a persecuted Jew, who experienced the increasing loss of rights first-hand, to the point where he himself was threatened with deportation. This coincided with the destruction of his hometown, Dresden's downfall in a firestorm, which saved his life. The fruits of my work gathering facts on the Nuremberg trials, on the other hand, was limited. Nevertheless, it had the function of opening the poison cabinets to the otherwise censored publications from the West. I was able to study Eugen Kogon (*The SS State*), Telford Taylor, Joe Heydecker and the twelve-volume series of writings of the International Military Court, all the monographs available then on the crimes committed in the concentration camps, the ghettos in the East and behind the fronts. Unfortunately, not yet Raul Hilberg's key work, *The Destruction of the European Jews*, which appeared in America as early as 1961 but in Germany, tellingly, only twenty years later. Claude Lanzmann's documentary film *Shoah* was still far beyond all horizons of such 'reappraisal'. It was through him that I first learnt the Hebrew word for the deflated term 'Holocaust'.

The result, then, was meagre compared with the wealth of specialized material available today. I, however, had been bitten by the bug of historical research, and my work soon began to display worryingly manic features.

For it didn't stop at that one assignment, it kept on expanding, until it took up three whole history lessons—to the great satisfaction of the teacher, who believed my soul had been saved for the anti-Fascist cause. In the end, I was pretty much clued up about the arms industry and the murderous judiciary in the Third Reich, about Hitler's euthanasia programme and the special task forces, the system of forced labour, the extermination camps and the medical experiments performed on inmates (Josef Mengele).

I can well imagine what a strange impression a fifteen-year-old must have made lecturing the class on racial politics, Jewish persecution, SS massacres, gas chambers and the role of German companies in the business of extermination. That was when I first learnt with absolute certainty that the firm I. G. Farben supplied Zyklon B, that the Erfurt company Topf & Sons built the crematoria and that the Allianz AG insurance company insured the barracks of Auschwitz.

And even today, immediately on waking, I could still recite the new categories established during the trials, against all precedent of jurisprudence:

Crimes against humanity,
war crimes and, most astonishingly:
crimes against peace.

Valid to this day, though often disregarded, is the Nuremberg out-lawing of the war of aggression. It was then, almost as an aside, that I first heard about the Declaration of Human Rights. But that was just one of the points that the dour teacher allowed to pass without comment. For the declaration touched on a taboo in the self-image of the other German state, because invoking universal human rights was the last resort of the opposition. The argument as to whether the GDR was an illegitimate state still divides people today. The Nuremberg trials, I explained to my classmates, were not a case of so-called victors' justice, and that, too, remained uncon-tradicted. Or had it simply been lost in the mass of material? Fired up by my awakening sense of justice, I was able to quote the American chief prosecutor, Judge Robert H. Jackson without challenge: 'That four great nations, flushed with victory and stung with injury stay the hand of vengeance and voluntarily submit their captive enemies to the judgement of the law is one of the most significant tributes that Power has ever paid to Reason.'

This was a completely new principle, and it sounded so auspi-ciously redolent of the values of a liberal order that even today, remembering the scene, I am still astonished by the silence in the classroom. It was as if the nations that held court over the mass murderers and their superiors had wanted for the first time to test out what Franz Kafka (in his diaries) had called 'jumping out of death row'. And for me it was as if I had won a small victory when the teacher, changing the habits of a lifetime, graded the lecture with an A+, because she could do nothing else. I still recall her fixing her gaze on me like a strange toad and me staring straight back.

Eleven years later, my first volume of poetry appeared, a year before the Soviet empire began to crumble with the fall of the Berlin Wall. *Grauzone morgens* (Mornings in the Grayzone) was the title, a book in which scenes like the ones just described added to the overall panorama, but which was more of a search image—you wouldn't find any of the crucial terms in it. Viewed today, one can see it followed the scenography of a Tarkovsky film. I happened to see his masterpiece *Stalker* in a Dresden cinema in the early '80s, but only later found the key to his enigmatic film parable in T. S. Eliot's *The Waste Land*: 'Who is the third who walks always beside you?' 'There is always another one walking beside you'. Only now am I fully aware of the overlapping motifs. Someone had been walking beside me for a long time. An angel? A superior?

One of my poems from that time reminds me of those days, and my trips to the Saxon Library.

'ACCEPT IT'

So many days with nothing
        occurring, nothing but those
brief winter manoeuvres, a few

mounds of snow in the mornings,
        melted away by evening, and the
strange moment at the barracks

was an exotic handbill: this little
   squad of Russian soldiers in
green felt uniforms, standing in silence

guarding a bundle of newspapers, and I read
   'коммунист' on top and
the line came into my mind: 'picture

the wristwatch on Jackson Pollock's wrist.'

It is no longer the spectre of Communism that haunts Europe today. It is the afterimage of authoritarian rule, the dream of right-wing populism among the people, realizable through propaganda and political marketing. All those discredited socialist utopias that vanished with the fall of the Soviet Union have been replaced by backward-looking visions of a strong nation with fortified borders and as self-sufficient an economy as possible. Regressive fantasies stoke the flames of the struggle for majorities (Rassemblement National is the name in France, before that Front National). Aggressive discourses of power that have long since captured command positions here and there in Europe and America. The theatrical spectacle starring real-estate tycoon T, the Twitter King Ubu Roi at the White House may soon be over, but it has shown where things might be heading in this second millennium.

'Retrotopia' was what the sociologist Zygmunt Baumann called this in his last, posthumously published, book; his critique of a world of nationalist politics that leads of necessity to a restricted sense of nationhood, to trade wars and the rearmament of the nuclear powers, in short: to the increasing violence to be seen in all spheres, first and foremost in language. Baumann knew what he was talking about, as a Jew he had experienced political violence early on, he too became an émigré in his thinking. It is hardly an accident that, after much back and forth between East and West, Baumann who had been born in Poznan (Poland) finally fetched up in England and died there having found a haven for the time being. The fixation on the past identified in his study rests on the need for security for the many uprooted people in Western societies. For these people freedom is simply overwhelming: the freedom of the individual as well as that of capital, that dissolves all ties and thus threatens the very basis of their existence. The discomfort with culture goes hand in hand with a transfiguration of the past. The 'little people', so his argument runs, want a return to the tribal fire, as if they had not failed more than once in that undertaking. In times of globalization and the migration that comes with it, phenomena generally experienced as a threat, and bringing with them the destabilization and dissolution of local and family life, with growing economic inequality and diffuse terrorism permeating all situations of everyday life, the visions arise from what he calls 'the lost/stolen/abandoned, but undead past, instead of being tied to the not-yet-unborn and so inexistent future'.

> But what kind of past is that?
> Past that doesn't pass by
> Past that has been overcome
> Past that has not been overcome.
> Memory, work of mourning,
> So many pasts that each one of us
> caught up in the whirl remembers differently
> But it's supposed to be just one

the good one, easily told,
ideally the one where everything was fine
Without the masses of the dead
Without those who went under the wheels
the murdered, those who died miserably
for whom there was no past
and often not even a grave
'Doesn't a breath of the air that pervaded
earlier days caress us as well?'

That was the idea of history:

In any given situation it is the last stage of time handed down
and passed on, or the most recent episode of the Great Narrative
in the form of a television series. It is the reassuring intermediate
state in which the lives of the living rest on the works of the dead,
and everything that has been passed down is at the disposal of the
most recent-comers.

An extreme form of Fascism: the destruction of the past in the
course of the struggle for the survival of the strongest (fittest), the
apotheosis of vitalism, pure technocracy riding roughshod over the
interests of human beings. The commemoration only of one's own
dead, to whom monuments and mausoleums are erected. The
march to the Weimar Republic began at the Feldherrenhalle.
When the hour of victory had struck, the 'leaders' of the new
Europe came together before the new temples for the commemo-
rative tryst, hands covering their privates. Fascism: 'One reason it
has a chance is that, in the name of progress, its opponents treat it
as a historical norm' (Walter Benjamin). 'The current amazement

that the things we are experiencing are *still* possible in the twentieth century is *not* a philosophical amazement.'

We should not, we are told, be tempted into drawing comparisons in order to understand what is happening today. We do not have to look to old models of explanation, nor does the reference to the emergence of National Socialism help us. But it may be pertinent to reflect on a few characteristics of classical Fascism in order to rule out the possibility that we are dealing with spectres of its return, or even simply derivatives of them, new chemical compounds, that could be produced out of old elements.

It is certainly not wrong to see Fascism as a politics of dynamism (its synonym was the Movement after all—'Munich, Capital of the Movement'). In addition to its original history of violence, it was the idea and formation of the masses powered by the most modern technological means, especially communication technology, today one would say a marketing strategy. Opponents were deported to the concentration camps, potential comrades brainwashed by Goebbels' propaganda, the Jews were excluded as foreign bodies and finally destroyed (this, however, was unique). Class hatred was replaced with racial hatred.

Historians deal with content and process; sociologists enquire into the impact on the structure of everyday life; philosophers concern themselves with the ideas involved and place them in the larger perspective of human thinking. There is agreement on the fact that it was a revolution—a revolution of the right, the only one that has ever really worked in Germany and caught the imagination of the people. In comparing two totalitarian movements, Fascism and Communism, the German historian Ernst Nolte sought to provoke and remained a lone voice. But no one can escape the shift

of perspective. Anyone who interprets this move, as the philosopher Habermas did during the 'historians quarrel', as a sign of revisionism is right in a humanist sense, but it stands in the way of a proper understanding of political dialectics. The two dragons of Communism and Fascism faced each other off snorting with rage. For a time, they competed on the world stage in terms of civilization and aesthetics (as is strikingly visible in the 1937 Paris World Fair), until their totalitarian flirtation descended into war.

But the question, as to which dragon was the more successful at courting the masses, leads us straight back to the present and to a decision. And this is where Umberto Eco comes in with his list of 'Common Features of Eternal or Ur-Fascism', delivered in a speech marking the fiftieth anniversary of Europe's liberation from Nazism at Columbia University and later expanded into a tract: *Il fascimo eterno.*

The semiotician takes the broad view without really resolving the contradictions: on the one hand, Fascism is, for him, part of the cult of tradition, a rejection of modernity ('blood and soil', fixation on race, condemnation of materialism and the 'evils of democracy', apotheosis of the *Führer*-state, Julius Evola); on the other hand, it relies on the most modern technology and, over time, even adopts an avant-garde approach, like its vanguard, the artists of Futurism. On the one hand, he claims, it is a mythical construction; on the other hand, a praxis, based on action for action's sake and thus materialist through and through. It exploits natural fears about social disparity (not so much based on income but rather background and religion) and sharpens them to their most pointed form. It arises out of frustration on a social or individual level: Hitler, the humiliated nobody, who would have so liked to become an artist. But there is a difference between *Mein Kampf* and *Anton Reiser*, the psychological novel by Karl Philipp Moritz.

This much is certain: it is a product of nationalism compounded until it is limitless, that is to say, *the exploitation of people based on the simple fact of being born in a country where they grew up and were unable to leave* (because poverty kept them prisoner). Jews who had lived there for generations, for their part permanent exiles, must remain outsiders forever. Who is an outsider and who belongs to the holy community prepared to give their lives for the nation, is determined by Fascism. Jews have been the eternal nomads since the time of Babylon; it is up to them to see where in the world they end up. Fascism is the construction of belonging, the identity of the Volk, including its own people living abroad, beyond its frontiers (those in Saarland, Sudeten, Romanian Germans and Volga Germans, etc.).

It is the ideology of the have-nots, who interpret capitalism as a conspiracy of plutocrats, i.e., millionaires (preferably Jews), but one which can only sustain itself through investment and campaign contributions on the part of big business. It postulates the struggle for survival and a cult of the strong (invoking Darwin in the process) and doesn't give a damn if the weak go under the wheels (the tank chains) or drown in the sea. It believes in the idea of a 'final solution' for all human problems: away with the weak, sick (homeless and mad), and any intransigent opponents. A constant war is to be fought, but in the end a Golden Age will dawn in which the biologically superior (not the most intelligent) lead an orderly family life. It dreams of an elite, but its foot soldiers come from the uneducated levels of society—intellectuals, the educated, the cultured are despised ('The Lying Press'). Fascism needs heroes, and they must be prepared to go above and beyond, they train for death, the final battle, and fight to the last cartridge. Fascism is a male affair. In the will to battle, women become mere accessories. In Fascism the situation of a woman is always precarious: there at best to become the bearer of children and heroic mother (by all means, a concentration-camp supervisor). Or even a deputy, a congresswoman in the right-wing populist camp, opponent of abortion. Never a feminist, in any case.

I must confess that for some time now, more than much else, I too have been concerned with the issue of the nostalgic appeal of Fascism. Has the spectre really been banished and burnt like the poor witches of the Middle Ages? The very thought: can you in fact burn spectres, as the Nazis burnt books on Berlin's Opernplatz?

Is there a myth that has remained alive—preserved under the rubble of the 'Thousand-Year Reich'—that may yet one day resurface? Heiner Müller: 'as once ghosts came from the past / now they come from the future as well.' For a long time, I considered such fear to be the product of hysteria but now I am not so sure. The theme of the return of the past only seemed relevant inasmuch as it was also gaining traction among historians and sociologists. Surely the experts had to be in a position to say what caused the virulence of these spectres. As long as they could assure me that we all found ourselves in a new situation and a revival of horrors, whether as farce or operetta, was ruled out historically, there was no danger.

It may be that it is the German in me that is gripped, every now and then, by a certain disquiet. That is why I stare as if trans-fixed at the twelve insane years of Nazi rule, constantly immerse myself in the growing specialist literature on the subject. Just recently yet another a new discovery concerning the generation of young career-makers in the Third Reich, Hitler's intelligent arm-chair perpetrators, the strategists of the time, educated, hard-work-ing, forward-looking. I came across the biography of a certain Franz Alfred Six. He was one of the co-founders of the Security Service (SD) in what became the Reich Main Security Office (RSHA) and was the ideal henchman to his boss Heinrich Himmler and a resourceful colleague of his almost contemporary and supe-rior Reinhard Heydrich, who was rumoured in the inner circles of the SS to be the heir apparent to Hitler. There are newspapers and there are newspaper readers, but one day, this is the imperative of self-regulating modernity, there also had to be a science of jour-nalism. One of its pioneers was that very same Franz Six, director of the Königsberg Institute of Journalism. In 1935 his position as major in the SS had nudged him ahead of his colleagues and he had been appointed head of the Press Department at the main office of the Security Service in Berlin; his specialty was research into *ideological opponents*. It was his office that gathered the huge stream of data concerning all those within Germany and abroad who, whether as organizers or publicists, could be defined as political opponents of the Nazi regime.

This would have been the man earmarked for the position of Commander of Security Police in London after the occupation of Britain, according to the wishes of his boss Heydrich. The order came personally from Field Marshal Göring. In the event of a successful invasion (Operation 'Sea Lion'), not only did all the operational plans of the various services lie ready in the cupboard, but also the lists of all potential opponents to be found on the island. From his counterpart SS Brigadier Walter Schellenberg comes the manual for the planned German invasion, which is the infamous *Sonderfahndungsliste G.B.* (special wanted list GB) that fell into the hands of the Allies after the end of the war. It had come into being mainly thanks to the diligence of the pedantic researcher Franz Six and his collaborators. Among the approximately 2,700 dangerous subjects to be arrested after the invasion (right at the top Winston Churchill as enemy No. 1) are the names Albert Einstein and Sigmund Freud, but also artists and writers like John Heartfield, Aldous Huxley, H. G. Wells, Virginia Woolf.

Franz Six was the typical armchair perpetrator, an inconspicuous civil servant, presumably often in plainclothes, with the international daily newspapers in his briefcase. He would hardly have stood out at a meeting of stamp collectors, with his round nickel-framed glasses. The fact that he had soon risen to a position that earned him a villa in Berlin-Dahlem (on Thielallee), a chauffeured

service car and a private office in the city centre with three secretaries (Wilhelmstrasse, Prinz-Albrecht-Palais) is a testament to the enormous opportunities for advancement in the dynamic Nazi state, whose inner workings the ordinary German people could hardly envisage. Six was the author of essays with titles such as 'The Fate of the European Community' or 'Russia as Part of Europe', but his core business was the creation of comprehensive catalogues of opponents. The walls of his Berlin office were papered with detailed organizational charts in which the world was divided into political groups presenting a threat. He shared with his superior Heydrich the fascination for a certain secret-service aura, copied wholesale from their British opponents.

His ambitious project was to coordinate domestic propaganda with so-called foreign studies, geopolitics and research into the various categories of opponent (Marxists, Socialists, Jews, Freemasons, Jesuits and members of religious sects) on the basis of a 'scientific National Socialism' postulated by him, analogous to the ideology of the revolutionary Bolsheviks. The concept of a branch of sociologically and historically defined research into the enemy came from none other than Reinhard Heydrich, the 'man with the iron heart', as Hitler dubbed his chief functionary at the pompous funeral ceremony after the successful assassination attempt on the Reich Governor of Bohemia and Moravia. Like his boss Himmler, he was also convinced that he was exposed to a huge and disparate army of potential opponents, after the occupation of half of Europe in a territory 'with 200 million people of foreign origin and race' (Himmler's speech to the assembled Reichs- and Gauleiter in Poznan in 1943). 'To win their hearts and minds will only be possible when the great struggle between the two world empires, Germany and England, is decided. Then we will be able to affiliate these 30 million true Teutons to our own nation.'

Thankfully, it never came to an invasion of Britain. Instead, England was to be worn down by air raids until it would agree to peace terms so that the Nazis could finally turn to Russia: the most serious competition for dominance in Europe. After the attacks on the Soviet Union, we see Herr Six at work once again. With his own motorized SS command, he drives just behind the advancing front to be the first of the security police in Moscow and to secure official archives and files from enemy authorities.

In the last years of the war, he is transferred to the Foreign Office, drives right across Europe, and as eye-witnesses attest, spends his time barking at employees of the diplomatic missions and cultural representatives. For his involvement in the crimes of task forces in Smolensk in the autumn of 1941, he was convicted in one of the smaller trials in Nuremberg but walked free again after four years in prison in Landsberg, uncorrected and undeterred. He never showed up on the list of spiritual fathers of Jewish extermination and was overlooked by historians for many years. In connection with this type of person, people spoke of 'functional anti-Semitism'. The 'physical elimination of Eastern Jewry' was nonetheless important enough to him for him to give a lecture on it, though whether he ever got his hands dirty remains unclear. His name stands for bureaucratic preparation; he was one of many 'intellectuals', who prepared the ground for annihilation. He stands here for an abbreviation, a seemingly fleeting file note and a large amount of paper, which in the end led to the most extreme consequences.

After the war, he transfers without missing a beat to the automobile industry, as a self-employed management consultant. The specialist for lethal propaganda becomes one of the leading marketing experts of Porsche-Diesel Motorenbau GmbH. Untroubled by justice, he lives through the building of the Federal Republic and, in receipt of a handsome salary, offers his reflections on 'The Nature of Marketing'. An observation from Paul Celan seems apposite: 'The germ-free is the murderous, Fascism today lies in formal design.'

Is that the way German biographies are rounded off? Chance or necessity: this is the point at which the theme of these lectures comes together and reaches a close. It was George Weidenfeld, the founder of this series of Oxford Lectures, who was one of the first to recognize the continuity between Fascist propaganda and its later useful forms in civilian life, especially in marketing, in his study *The Goebbels Experiment* (1942). At that time, his was one of the first attempts to explore something that engages us still: the question of how opinions are manipulated by media in a mass society. Remember: Goebbels was the man who had studied German in Heidelberg, he had a way with words. And was as such 'an exception among the SS-bruisers' as Weidenfeld puts it in an interview with the German magazine *Der Spiegel*. 'In his own way he was a genius, intellectually and stylistically far more interesting, of course, than the uneducated or semi-educated Nazi leaders. What is more, he understood how to organize propaganda in a very modern way.' This is the nub. How can the message of hatred be rendered fresh and linguistically appealing and transported into the brains of the general public? Goebbels was the ready-made mouthpiece, a Nazi orator like none before him; demagogues all over the world will continue to learn from him in their training programmes.

What refuses to give me any peace is the way a people can make themselves totally available to an ideology. That it was specifically the German people in this case is something that concerns the world to this day. Why it was that the Germans under Hitler and the inhabitants of the Soviet Union under Stalin (made compliant by the revolution) were so dependent, and what their historical experience means will occupy us for a long time to come.

The question 'Who would you have been in a dictatorship?' is one I do not have to ask myself, because I found myself in the middle of one and survived it.

Instead, it is the question: who would you have been in the Nazi era, and what would you have done against Hitler, subject to the ubiquitous images and words of the *Führer*? At the time there was no outside vantage point, so there is no point in developing a moral standpoint with the benefit of hindsight. The principle of contemporaneity, to which we are bound, excludes us from other historical experiences. All I can say is that as a young child I had slept through all knowledge of the Third Reich; and someone could have called out to me: keep on dreaming, friend. So, the only question can be: can anything be learnt from this particular history, indeed can anything ever be learnt from the course of history?

Now I am emerging into the present. Now I am rising to the surface of our times in full consciousness. But I would like to come back, in conclusion, to the problem of writing and the question of why one writes in the first place. Most people do not ask themselves the question quite so urgently: why live without writing? I know this of course, but it was a question for me from early on. You wander silently within yourself for a long time before you get to the point of scribbling a few lines on a piece of paper, at first only for yourself and naturally without the least understanding of history.

Let's hear what the philosopher Gilles Deleuze has to say about it. 'Writing is a question of becoming, always incomplete, always in the midst of being formed, and goes beyond the matter of any liveable or lived experience.' That is the starting point: we don't know what is driving us, and we can only pull together a few phrases to express what happens to us—to form a provisional response. Writing will sum us up, it shortens what we call life, quite inevitably. The philosopher, Deleuze, standing before the Absolute ('Literature and Life'), then makes leaps and bounds, he is immediately in need of transforming himself—into a woman, into an animal, a plant, a molecule—and he is right. 'The shame of being a man—is there any better reason to write?'

127

No, there is no better reason, and I will skip over his other thoughts on the subject and stop at a statement that immediately seized me and would not let go of me when I read his *Essays Critical and Clinical* (1993) for the first time. 'As Moritz said, one writes for the dying calves.' He was referring to Karl Philipp Moritz, a writer of the Goethe period, author of *Anton Reiser*, a life story told from below, from the perspective of a child born into poverty and a strict religious milieu, the first *psychological novel* in the German language.

Deleuze had simply provided the cue, but I was electrified and followed the trail—and: I came out at myself. My first narrative text, the first one I worked on seriously, started at a street crossing in Dresden, I was sixteen at the time. After visiting my grandparents, I was waiting for the tram that was supposed to take me back to the outskirts of the city, to that garden city of Hellerau, where we had been living for a few years. So, I was standing there, staring out into the rain that had just started, when a cattle truck roared past me. I will never forget the sight of the animals, the dark eyes of the cows and calves, the bodies of those destined for death, clearly visible behind the vents of the van. This is where my text began.

It was the monologue of a cow being taken to the slaughterhouse. Written in a primitive stream-of-consciousness style (interior monologue). I did not know James Joyce or Arthur Schnitzler at the time. I knew nothing of the fact that literature was also a technique that could be learnt, developed. With that momentary glance, the glint of a pupil, I had recognized myself in this animal, and the prose began to flow. The piece almost wrote itself. It ended after all the stress and terror of being unloaded on the ramp and driven through a tunnel towards the last station of its suffering, with the moment the beast felt the bolt gun pressed against its forehead. I knew the procedure because my grandfather, who spent his life working as a master butcher in the Dresden slaughterhouse, had once told me about it.

As the ill-treated creature blacked out, the text suddenly broke off. Quite clearly: an unsatisfactory ending for a story. And I felt my failure acutely and buried the manuscript under other half-baked drafts, overcome with a feeling of shame. I was upset because nothing seemed to work. That is the painful secret of writing—I do not know what to expect, just as a laboratory animal in the midst of an experiment on himself does not know where the exploration will lead. 'To write is not to recount one's memories and travels, one's loves and griefs, one's dreams and fantasies.' That I had understood very quickly. '. . . Literature begins only when a third person is born in us that strips us of the power to say I,' as Deleuze put it. But even without such an 'I', I was stuck for a long time. 'Health as literature, as writing, consists in inventing a people who are missing.' Deleuze's phrase sounded pompous, but one day it dawned on me what it meant—and so, more or less by chance, I fell into German literature as one of many who dream of a people that does not yet exist.

'You write for the dying calves, says Moritz.' I had read the novel with that sentence early on but only came across the specific reference thanks to a French philosopher. It is there, but not in quite the same words. That can happen if one simply reads. It is not about the reading itself; it is about stopping at a certain point. And that was it, the point I had simply passed over.

From this time forward, when he saw an animal slaughtered, he identified himself with it in thought, and as he so
often had the opportunity of seeing it at the slaughterer's,
for a long time his thought was centred on this—to arrive
at the distinction between himself and a slaughtered animal
like that. He often stood for an hour, looking at a calf's
head, eyes, ears, mouth, and nose—and, pressing as close to
it as possible, as he did with a human stranger, often with
the foolish fancy that it might be possible for him to think
himself gradually into the nature of the animal. His own
concern was to know the difference between himself and
the animal; and sometimes he forgot himself so completely
as he gazed at it persistently that for a moment he really
believed he had come to feel the nature of the *creature's exis-*
tence. From childhood on his thoughts were busy with the
question—how would it be if I were for instance a dog or
some other animal living among men?

From the philosophers, above all Descartes, who saw animals
as machines, bundles of reflexes, creatures without reason, one can
learn what a discourse is. Literature has always had its own discourses and themes. In this it has always been sovereign and did
not need to wait for the social sciences. If asked about my poetics,
I would say today: we are working towards a photosynthesis of
words and images. Words work at transmission; images reach us
from a tiny future that quickly becomes the past. That is, the images
in all media that overwhelm us every day as a shock experience of
the real, right down to our dreams. Every day, history drives us out
of ourselves and confuses our imagination: history—that brutal
translation of time into collective experience. The poet is simply one

of many, his problem is how to lay aside the pretentions of poetry. In the end he only knows what anyone could know: there are so many realities, they exist independently of us and simultaneously, and the same is true of identities. Even if they are dreamers, the poets, the only thing they do not doubt is that the words and deeds of our predecessors will catch up with us. In this respect they are sensitive, specialists, constantly in radio contact with the dead.

There is something the sociologists call transgenerational transmission. No one can jump out of their historical time, no one escapes being formed by history. Once perhaps in the unimaginable times of myth and fairy tale, but today it is impossible. In the same way, the much-vaunted attempt to draw a line under legacy of German fascism is impossible too.

There is no question of a flight from time, nor a flight inwards— for even there, history will catch up with everyone. Instead, history as a history of violence passes though time and imprints itself with all its dates on our bodies. There is something beyond literature that calls writing into question. And there is literature that criss-crosses history in fictions, literature as a 'secret agreement between the past generations and the present one'.

'Doesn't a breath of the air that pervaded earlier days caress us as well? In the voices we hear, is there not an echo of now silent ones?' asks Walter Benjamin. 'History constantly teaches but it finds no disciples', responds Ingeborg Bachmann, who has it from Antonio Gramsci.

She had experience with this, no doubt: she was a woman. But we cannot know; fortunately, we cannot know, whether this is the last word on the matter.

NOTES AND REFERENCES

'THE VIOLET POSTAGE STAMP'

Adolf Hitler, *Mein Kampf, Volume 2* (Munich, 1932); *Mein Kampf* (Ralph Manheim trans.) (Boston, MA: Houghton Mifflin Harcourt, 1998).

Edmund Kalb, *Leben und Werk* (Cologne: Walther König, 2014).

Friedrich Percyval Reck-Malleczewen, *Tagebuch eines Verzweifelten* (Bonn: Dietz 1981); *Diary of a Man in Despair* (Paul Rubens trans.) (London, Duck Editions, 2000).

Konrad Heiden, *Adolf Hitler: Das Zeitalter der Verantwortungslosigkeit* (Zurich: Europaverlag, 1936).

Vladimir Nabokov, *Speak Memory: An Autobiography Revisited* (New York: Everyman's Library; Alfred A. Knoff, 1999[1947]).

'LANDSCAPE IN FETTERS'

Piero Puricelli, 'Entwurf für ein europäisches Autostraßennetz', *Zeitschrift Die Straße, Organ des Generalsinspektors für das deutsche Straßenwesen* 2 (Berlin, 1934).

'To imagine Europe, is to imagine it covered with an integrated and organic network of motorway connections, that following the movement of the greatest amount of traffic, result in a closed transport system that meets the requirements of the age.' (Piero Puricelli, 'Design for a European Road Network', 1934)

Fritz Todt, 'Der Sinn des neuen Bauens', *Die Straße* 4 (Berlin, 1937).

Stanley McClatchie, *Look to Germany: The Heart of Europe* (Berlin: Verlag Heinrich Hoffmann, 1937).

Friedrich Kittler, 'AUTO BAHNEN', in *Explosion of a Memory, Heiner Müller DDR Ein Arbeitsbuch* (Berlin: Edition Hentrich, 1988).

Siegfried Kracauer, *Totalitäre Propaganda* (Bernd Stiegler ed., with Maren Neumann and Joachim Heck) (Frankfurt am Main: Suhrkamp, 2013).

Achievements of the Reichsautobahn project in the years of the Weimar Republic: in the spirit of Bauhaus architecture, it provided the first solutions for the technical problems involved in the new overland road construction. For example, the separation of oncoming traffic by means of a central reservation, a 'cloverleaf interchange' for motorway intersections, even an early concept for landscaping and integrating the highway into the natural environment was already there on paper.

Among the pioneers in this field was the architect **Mies van der Rohe,** who raised the 'question of the artistic problem of the Autobahn' beyond the usual low-cost solutions driven by pressure from advertising agencies on behalf of investment companies, which conceived of the Autobahn only as a large and permanently available advertising hoarding, like those in the sports' stadiums. 'When we speak of giving special attention to the landscape, it goes without saying that under no circumstances should the usual advertising along the side of the road be allowed.'

The first designs for practical Reichsautobahn SERVICE STATIONS came from the drawing board of Mies van der Rohe. Two of them were brought into being in Hanover even before the Nazis' general plans got underway. They fulfilled their function right up until the 1970s before giving way to the new Aral and Shell stations. They were the typical flat roof constructions beloved of cool modernity, *radical chic*, and thus from the beginning a thorn in the side of the foremen of the Third Reich with their folksy construction fantasies. After the Nazis took power, the so-called Heimatschutzstil (homeland-preservation style) determined construction design the length of the Autobahn. From now on, all rest stops, motorway depots, even petrol stations were camouflaged with traditional German construction styles, adapted to local conditions, decorated with greenery, each of them a tavern in the Spessart hills. A style rooted in German fairy tale came to dominate, and the unadulterated traditions of *Heimat* became big business. Buildings were constructed with native limestone, mountain-style refuges with high gabled roofs were in demand.

That PARALLELS meet at infinity suddenly seemed almost tangible. On a portion of flat road, it looked as if the dead-straight lines of the carriageways might finally converge. Planners discussed multistorey roads. An extreme case is the two-storey motorway on the Salzburg–Villach–Klagenfurt route. Viaducts were used, gradually opening onto the view of the mountain landscape. The problem of intersections also had to be solved, often many kilometres in advance. Overpasses and underpasses were considered, including the clearance gauge, intended to moderate the effects of moving directly from zones of shadow into daylight. This was how they set about achieving the desired gliding rhythm, which drivers nowadays take for granted and which serves to shorten the duration of long-distance journeys, during which all the bodily sensations inspired by normal hormonal cycles are experienced as if in fast forward.

Wilhelm Reich, *Die Massenpsychologie des Faschismus* (Copenhagen, Prague and Zurich: Verlag für Sexualpolitik, 1933); *Mass Psychology of Fascism* (Theodore P. Wolf trans.) (New York: Orgone Institute, 1946).

Albert Speer, 'Der Baumeister Fritz Todt', *Deutsche Technik. Die technopolitische Zeitschrift* 10 (1942).

A whole chapter of the planning regime was in and of itself dedicated to TUNNELS. The first practical test was the so-called 'Nasenfelstunnel' on the route between Stuttgart and Ulm. The largest aperture driven through the rock was the Engelberg Tunnel on the motorway between Heilbronn and Stuttgart. Instead of removing the rock, it was decided to create a route through it in the fashion of a mining project. Natural obstacles, of whatever kind, were overcome in ways dependent on the local circumstances—the overriding principle was no interruption, the traffic on the concrete production line had to be maintained at all costs. They key was always to exploit the velocity of the vehicle: ' . . . [W]hen the Autobahn descends from altitude, crosses a short deep valley and rises again on the other slope.' And further in the lively engineering German of that time: 'Descending in a straight line allows the Autobahn to glide over all obstacles in its way with a single swooping motion, which creates *images of unique power and beauty.*'

New techniques pioneered in motorway construction mainly concerned the MANUFACTURING PROCESS: for example, the 'Delmag frogs', pile-rammers that flattened the ground with pneumatic tampers. This was a formidable machine that rolled forward on wide iron railroad tracks, operated by several skilled workers with shovels and poles. In a single operation it managed to tread down the upper layer of material, which was then smoothed and polished. This was the prototype out of which the so-called road paver was developed, a universal machine that could produce both substructure and surface that is 'the entire road, without any additional machine or manual labour'. Among the labourers, the monster was nicknamed 'the worker bee'. It was followed by the paving screed machine, a device unpopular with labourers, that helped rework the whole thing at 150 beats a minute and made the operators' weak human bodies vibrate.

Heinrich Mann, *Der Hass* (Amsterdam: Querido, 1933).

Annie Ernaux, *The Years* (Alison L. Strayer trans.) (London: Fitzcarraldo, 2017).

The sociological epic of Western society in the second half of the twentieth century was written by a woman. A consistent auto-sociology, against the background of which the psychological contours of the person reporting emerge all the more clearly. For the first time we see justice done to the ordinary life of a contemporary person in an ongoing chronicle. Holding a mirror up to one's own culture until all the traits of the community resolve into a recognisable individual was the concept: looking at oneself and one's peers and our way of life in the same way as the ethnologists used to do with foreign tribes was the author's aim. She achieved it in a ground-breaking way.

A postscript from a contemporary viewpoint. Serious ACCI-DENTS also increased as the motorways were built. The rain-slicked carriage ways and the ever-increasing speed of the new vehicles meant they were inevitably part of the overall picture. There was hardly anyone who had not already had a brush with death after hours of racing along on the multi-lane highways, especially in the vicinity of construction sites that never seem to come to an end. Unforgettable scenes of horror featuring mass pile-ups, overturned lorries and desperate victims dancing around a warning triangle were now commonplace—until the oil crisis arrived, bringing it all to a temporary halt.

Robert Ley, 'Vom Wesen des ständischen Aufbaus', *National-sozialistische Monatshefte* 42 (1933).

Victor Klemperer, *Ich will Zeugnis ablegen bis zum letzten. Tagebücher 1933–1945* (Berlin: Aufbau, 1995); *I Will Bear Witness, 1942–1945: A Diary of the Nazi Years*, VOL. 2 (Martin Chalmers trans.) (New York: Random House, 2001).

Gottfried Benn, *Briefe an Elinor Büller (1930–1937)* (Stuttgart: Klett-Cotta, 1992).

Despite any Expressionist critique of modernity, the poet was completely open to technical innovation. In 1933, when the future in the new Nazi state still seemed bright to him, almost Greek (the 'Doric world'), he had proudly welcomed the futurist Filippo Marinetti, a speed fanatic and passionate motorist from the very off, at a reception in the Prussian Academy and greeted him as a fellow spirit. This was a man entirely to his taste, an impressive and artistic aristocrat. Suddenly here was the chance to be able to court a true avant-gardist, as the official cultural ambassador of Italy, the trailblazer among fascist states. Marinetti, the son of a wealthy lawyer, had been among the few in Milan who could afford a motor car of their own. In the first Futurist Manifesto of 1909, announced in Paris, with the instinct of the born advertising expert, in the country's most important newspaper, *Le Figaro*, a jaunt with friends through Milan at night became a foundational experience for him. Marinetti describes the feeling that every motoring-fanatic in his powerful vehicle will recognize. 'We went over to the three snorting beasts to stroke their hot breasts. I stretched out in my car like a corpse on a stretcher, but immediately awoke to new life under the steering wheel that threatened my stomach like a guillotine.' Two cyclists come towards him on an empty road, he jams on the brakes, goes into a tailspin and ends up in the nearest ditch. A lucky escape. The open-top car, today a vintage model gathering dust in the museums of technology, escaped with a few scratches. The defeat, however, was quickly styled a victory. The sensation of driving is what triumphs: that pulses through his body and still trembles within it.

A primal experience told in the style of the apostle stories: initiation of modern man into the delirium of speed. The artist proclaims the gospel of all future avant-gardes. In fact, Marinetti was the born Formula One driver. His manifesto set the tone in which the public was informed of advances in the field of art from now on. Euphorically, the poet welcomes the overcoming of space and time. 'Death at the Wheel' was the title of a prose poem; he was the first to celebrate of the wild chase of motor races. But on that night in Milan, he hung like a beetle stuck in his chitin armour.

Once again, antiquity in the form of Nike of Samothrace had triumphed over a screeching car. A scene from a silent film is described: 'As I crawled out like a dirty, smelly rag from under my upturned car, I felt an invigorating stab of joy penetrate my heart like a red-hot poker!' This sets in motion of one of the most significant art movements of the new century. It will soon throw in its lot with Fascism. Mussolini is the politician who answers the call, right on cue, to translate the Futurist programme and its obsession with the technical into reality: abolition of the past, the cursed *passato*, in which Italy, the land of antiquity, had been trapped for so long, as a pilgrimage centre for mass tourism; the storming of the libraries, museums and archives; the cult of the machine and work; a hymn of praise for a new, united Italy; completion of the *Risorgimento* and fervour for war. Even today, some still believe that it was only through Marinetti and his vicarious political agent, Mussolini, that Italy found the path to itself and the connection to modernity.

Otto Kurz, 'Zukünftige Landschaftsbilder an der Reichsautobahn', *Die Straße, Organ des Generalsinspektors für das deutsche Straßen-wesen* 19, *Beilage Die Autobahn* (Berlin, 1936).

For an example of the biological thinking at the time, and not without a certain provocation, take the following statement by the Reich Labour leader Konstantin Hierl: 'Service to German mothers is a service to public health, to German blood'. A clear injunction to all male workers, as to how to spend their next holiday in an appropriate manner. There is no pause in their work: even sexual intercourse is co-opted as part of the proper performance of their duties.

Dieter Wellershoff, *Der Ernstfall. Innenansichten des Krieges*
(Cologne: Kieopenheuer & Witsch, 1995)

Saul Friedländer, *Kitsch und Tod, Der Widerschein des Nazismus*
(Munich: DTV, 1986); *Reflections of Nazism: An Essay on Kitsch
and Death* (Thomas Weyr trans.) (Bloomington and Indianapolis: Indiana University Press, 1993).

In his study, Saul Friedländer describes a paralysis of language, a
linguistic block, that gripped the German literary landscape in the
wake of its being eclipsed by Nazism: ' . . . [E]vents moved more
quickly than language. Since Auschwitz the distance between them
seems unsurmountable.' And he adds a question which today seems
much more fundamental than W. G. Sebald's claim that Germans
has never dealt adequately with their own trauma in that they had
never found a literary form to work through the air war, the
destruction of German cities, nor those cities destroyed by the
Germans during the war: 'Is there a work of art, a work of literature,
for example, that has been able, in a decisive way, to confront these
events?'

Friedländer, the history teacher, articulates a critique of the dry
language of historians. Here we see him arguing out of personal
experience and against his own profession: his young parents had
placed their child in safety in a Catholic boarding school but were
sent back when they attempted to cross the Swiss border and were
deported from France to Auschwitz. His findings speak to the situation today in which the window of opportunity is closing for
good as the last concentration camp survivors are finally dying out.
'Revisionism purifies the past by trafficking in facts. At the opposite
extreme, systematic historical research, which uncovers the facts in

their most precise and most meticulous interconnection, also protects us from the past, thanks to the inevitable paralysis of language. That is the exorcism *and the involuntary evasion to which we are all subject* and whose mechanism has to be taken apart.'

Adam Zagajewski, *Asymmetry: Poems* (Clare Cavanagh trans.) (New York: Farrar, Straus and Giroux, 2018).

Gabriele Tergit, *Käsebier erobert den Kurfürstendamm* (Berlin: Rowohlt, 1932); *Käsebier Takes Berlin* (Sophie Duvernoy trans.) (New York: New York Review Books, 2019).

'THE AERIAL WAR OF IMAGES'

Hannah Arendt, *Ein Besuch in Deutschland 1950* (Berlin: Rotbuch Verlag, 1993); 'The Aftermath of Nazi Rule: Report from Germany', in *Essays in Understanding, 1930–1954: Formation, Exile, and Totalitarianism* (Jerome Kohn ed.) (New York: Schocken Books, 1994).

Take care with the slogan *barbarism*. Hannah Arendt: 'Incidentally, the mendacity starts with the word "barbarism" that is so popular in Germany today for the Hitler era; here, for example, it sounds as if Jewish and non-Jewish intellectuals turned their backs on a country that was no longer distinguished and educated enough for them.'

Peter Sieferle, *Finis Germania* (Schnellroda: Antaios Verlag, 2017).

Finis Germania is a posthumously published volume of essays by a retired professor of sociology who took his own life, a tragic testament to the confusion of a mind surrounded by collapsing historical perspectives. It contains the whole repertoire of those strategies—denial of guilt, national persecution complex, fear of foreign domination, fear of collapse—that have always characterized the thinking of neo-conservatives and new right—and now do so again today. Even taking on the role of victim belongs to the tried and tested rhetorical feints. 'People living in Germany, he claims, have had to become as accustomed to dealing with anti-German sentiment, as the Jews had to learn to come to terms with anti-Semitism'. Bizarrely enough, this slim volume, the private notes of a confused professor, ignited a debate about censorship and freedom of expression in the public media of the Federal Republic.

Max Horkheimer and Theodor W. Adorno, *Die Dialektik der Aufklärung* (Amsterdam: De Gruyter, 1947); *Dialectic of Enlightenment* (John Cumming trans.) (New York: Herder and Herder, 1972).

Ré Soupault, *Katakomben der Seele. Eine Reportage über West-deutschlands Vertriebenen- und Flüchtlingsproblem 1950* (Heidelberg: Verlag das Wunderhorn, 2016).

Heinrich Mann, *Der Hass* (Amsterdam: Querido, 1933).

Thomas Mann, *Vom zukünftigen Sieg der Demokratie* (Zurich and New York: Oprecht, 1938); *The Coming Victory of Democracy* (Agnes E. Meyer trans.) (New York: Alfred A. Knopf, 1938).

Waiting things out on the side-lines in Swiss exile, he had in the early years of the Hitler regime moved for a long time in a zone of neutrality. It had long been the wish of the Nobel Laureate to keep hold of his German audience. Although, in the year of Hitler's accession to power he had written to Albert Einstein, 'For me to have been driven into this role, truly unusually false and evil things had to happen, and in my opinion this *German Revolution* is truly false and evil.'

Andreas Petersen, *Die Moskauer. Wie das Stalintrauma die DDR prägte* (Frankfurt am Main: Fischer Verlag, 2019).

W. G. Sebald, *Luftkrieg und Literatur* (Munich: Hanser, 1999); *On the Natural History of Destruction* (Anthea Bell trans.) (New York: Random House, 2003).

Victor Klemperer, *LTI* (Berlin: Aufbau, 1947); *The Language of the Third Reich*: *LTI Lingua Tertii Imperii* (Martin Brady trans.) (London and New York: Continuum, 2006).

Gottfried Benn, *Doppelleben* (Wiesbaden: Limes, 1950); *Double Life* (Simona Draghici trans.) (Indianapolis: Plutarch Press, 2002).

Alexander Kluge, *Der Luftangriff auf Halberstadt am 8. April 1945* (Frankfurt am Main: Suhrkamp, 2008); *Air Raid: On Halberstadt on 8 April 1945* (Martin Chalmers trans.) (London: Seagull Books, 2014).

Erich Nossack, *Der Untergang* (Frankfurt am Main: Suhrkamp, 1962); *The End: Hamburg, 1943* (Joel Agee trans.) (Chicago: University of Chicago Press, 2004).

Edward Timms, *Anna Haag and Her Secret Diary of the Second World War: A Democratic German Feminist's Response to the Catastrophe of National Socialism* (New York: Peter Lang, 2016); *Die geheimen Tagebücher der Anna Haag: Eine Feministin im Nationalsozialismus* (Michael Pfginstl trans.) (Bad Vilbel: Scoventa, 2019). This is an extended version of the original English.

At one point she succeeds in creating a striking collage, simply by setting the bald facts down alongside one another and letting them speak for themselves. Under the date 12 December 1942, she writes about mothers whose sons are in the final school year. Quotation from Edward Timms: 'They [. . .] asked the teacher to fail their sons so that they had to repeat the year—and could thus postpone conscription.' This brings Haag to the question of whether 'the German people—led by German mothers—might again find their way back to real naturally grounded maternal instincts.' Just below she has pasted in a report cut out of a local newspaper: 'The Ghetto in Luck (Lutsk)'. It is an (extraordinarily revealing) piece about the clearing of the Jewish ghetto set up under German occupation.

'Now they have gone—' it declares before describing the hygienic conditions in the now empty ghetto in lurid terms: 'the sewage of a subhuman species for which there is no comparison on the whole continent'. On the opposite page of the diary there is one of the press images of the time. It shows Hitler in conversation with several of his generals accompanied by the Reich Minister for Armament, Albert Speer, who received a relatively mild sentence at the Nuremberg trials and was released after twenty years' imprisonment.

Virginia Woolf, *The Diary, Volume 5: 1936–1941* (Anne Olivier Bell ed., with Andrew McNeillie) (London: Hogarth Press, 1977); see also 'Thoughts on Peace in an Air Raid', *The New Republic*, 21 October 1940.

After the invasion of the Netherlands and Belgium, the Woolfs take the decision to die together if Germany's invasion of the British Isles (codename 'Sea Lion') should succeed. As if they knew about the plans of SS Commander Alfred Six, they were under no illusions about their fate. Leonard Woolf was a Jew and a socialist—and they knew, with occupied France before their eyes, that the Gestapo, who would arrive along with the German Wehrmacht, would take the same measures as they were now taking against the French Jews. In preparation for the worst-case scenario they procured poison and hoarded gasoline in their garage.

Heinz Bude, *Bilanz der Nachfolge. Die Bundesrepublik und der Nationalsozialismus* (Frankfurt am Main: Suhrkamp, 1992).

'FOR THE DYING CALVES'

Martin Heidegger, *Der Feldweg* (Frankfurt am Main: Kloster-mann, 1953); *Country Path Conversations* (Bret W. Davis trans.) (Bloomington, Indiana University Press, 2010).

Theodor W. Adorno, *Der Jargon der Eigentlichkeit* (Frankfurt am Main: Suhrkamp, 1964); *The Jargon of Authenticity* (Knut Tarnowski and Frederic Will trans) (Evanston, IL: North-western University Press, 1977).

Joseph Brodsky, 'Spoils of War', in *On Grief and Reason: Essays* (New York: Farrar, Straus and Giroux, 1995), pp. 3–21.

Joe Heydecker and Johannes Leeb, *Der Nürnberger Prozeß* (Frank-furt am Main: Büchergilde Gutenberg, 1979).

Raul Hilberg, *The Destruction of the European Jews* (revised and definitive edn), 3 VOLS (New York: Holmes and Meier, 1985).

Durs Grünbein, 'Accept It!', here translated by Karen Leeder; see also *Ashes for Breakfast: Selected Poems* (Michael Hofmann trans.) (New York: Farrar, Straus and Giroux, 2005).

'NOTE ON THE AXIS POWERS'

In Autumn 1937 Mussolini and Hitler meet for a demonstration of strength in Munich which has functioned as the 'Capital of the Movement' since Hitler's accession to power. They review a parade on Königsplatz in front of the local crowds, both of them in uni-form, military men hung with medals and badges of honour and surrounded by their similarly uniformed henchmen. Hitler has his hands crossed in front of his genitals like a football player in front of a penalty shot. They are trying to save face, staring straight ahead into the distance, as if they knew that a mountain of lies was building between them. They are orchestrating the image of themselves as guarantors of the peace that one of them has already broken and the other is about to break, to the horror of the world. The Duce may believe that things will work out this time. He feels he is called upon, as emperor, modern Augustus, inheritor of the old Roman Empire, to strike a deal for a balance of power with Germania for the sake of modern Italy. His people, squeezed in between Mount Etna and the Brenner Pass, fear the expansion of a greater Germany and a potential war that they know they will lose. He will not tolerate an annexation of Austria; he does not want the Germans breathing down their neck. The fact that he will soon have to accept this is the result of his own desire for adventure. The man from Braunau understands the fact that the Western powers have swallowed Mussolini's occupation of Abyssinia as a signal to move in on Vienna.

After the meeting they start the hectic building of defensive positions in the mountains. Today one can still visit the enormous systems of bunkers in the Tyrolian Alps. Mussolini feels he is the descendent of Emperor Augustus. He has just been formally declared his legitimate heir in the Mostra Augustea ceremony in the Palazzo delle Esposizioni in Rome. Fascism stands in the tradition of Augustan power; a fact testified to by the fasces on posters and flags and on the facades of all official buildings. In comparison, Hitler's propaganda with the swastika simply seems to belong to a historical parvenu.

Mussolini lifts his imperial chin while the German (who was never a German) struts proudly among his men like a capon puffing up his breast. Mistrusting the Germans, Mussolini will soon secure the borders in secret. Along the line where troops could enter, from Piedmont across to Trieste, a first line of defence must be drawn. Bunkers are built in the mountains; Alpine fortifications appear along the old passes running south. While road construction forges ahead, as everywhere in the German Reich, the demarcation line between him and his new comrade is fortified, cellars are built underneath with deep tunnels for a whole shadow army, artillery positions are poised to bombard the approach roads at the slightest movement from the north. The path of the new ally will be blocked if he arrives as an enemy; the newly built bridges will be destroyed by remote detonation; the hairpin bends will be blasted to pieces by machine-gun nests in case of betrayal. And betrayal is on the cards—they know each other too well already. Two bandits meet in Munich, Fascist leaders the pair of them; mincing around each other according to the rules of a medieval royal court. But in truth they are just mafia bosses in a modern Chicago; troglodytes engaged in a mating dance.

Afterwards they travel in Hitler's special train to the capital of the Reich, Berlin. Many press photos mark the occasion. I turn them over in my hands using a magnifying glass to search for traces of dissonance, cracks in the charade of mutual deception. This find leapt out of a shoe box of photographs and postcards at the Berlin flea market along the Strasse des 17. Juni. I could not resist, had to pluck it out of the stream of forgetting—there was nothing like it in the schoolbooks of my youth. And even later in the countless books about the policy of the 'axis powers' there was nothing anywhere near as expressive. No point immersing oneself in the documentaries that run on all the TV channels. You only really understand when you hold the documents in your own hands, as if for the first time. The postcard bears a date and a looping signature in black ink. On the back, an SA man, one of many who found their place in the ceremony, remembers the big day.

> In fond memory of my being part of the parade for the Duce and the *Führer*
>
> on 25 October 1937
>
> as the 3rd man in the first rank (of 12 rows) of the SA-group Hochland, marching past the two Honour Temples on the Königsplatz, Munich.
>
> Staff Sergeant F. G.
>
> Sturm 3/ S2, Munich
>
> I was on SA duty for the return of the Duce from Berlin as an auxiliary policeman at Munich South Railway Station for 22 and a half hours straight from 7 a.m. until 1 p.m. and then again until 5 a.m.

So, we see the absurd level of organization, the precision of the pomposity of this kind of State event calculated down to the very minute by someone who was proud to be a cog in the machine. What he could not see in his admiration for the whole ritual, filled as he was with the historical significance of the moment, was the jealous jostling of the rivals for power, the competition between the master and his apprentice, the courtship dance of two tyrants before the throng—the perfect opportunity for a comedian like Charlie Chaplin. In the news reels the Hollywood star found the raw material for his classic 1940 film, *The Great Dictator*. The message of the satire: Fascism was unintentionally comic, the projection of military might as musical comedy. Of course, only a Jew could

have the temerity to make fun of the *Führer*-state as guarantor of discipline and order. So it was that the impression took hold among a large swathe of his audience that Charlie Chaplin, the small, dark-haired actor in the double role of the Dictator Hynkel and the Jewish barber in a Polish ghetto, must himself be Jewish—a Jewish caricature for the world's anti-Semites. And he appeared a little later in *Der ewige Jude* (*The Eternal Jew*), one of the worst of the Nazi propaganda films, identified as Jewish. Scenes from his slapstick set pieces were supposed to illustrate the wretched atmosphere of the East European shtetl. My grandparents' generation believed that Chaplin, the little man with the ridiculously big shoes and ragged trousers, the mangy tramp, naturally had to be Jewish— what else could he be? A classic example of the effectiveness of prejudice. It is to his honour and says a good deal about the latitude enjoyed by the entertainer of yesteryear that he never denied the false identity.

In her essay 'Die verborgene Tradition' ('The Jew as Pariah: A Hidden Tradition'), Hannah Arendt identified this as the prime example of the hide-and-seek of the persecuted. For Arendt, Chaplin was the pariah par excellence. According to statements from close friends, Chaplin consciously allowed the rumour to circulate, as a stand against anti-Semitism, which, it seemed, could not be extinguished once and for all, even in America. The philosopher insisted on her interpretation right to the last and complained bitterly that Chaplin obstinately refused to be a Jew.

For someone like the Munich SA-man, the Chaplin film would have been a slap in the face. Would he have been able to understand that the whole thing was as comical as the elaborate preparations before an execution?

The government train arrives at the station of the capital of Tomainia; the ruler of Bacteria is expected. As the red carpet is rolled out, the choreography goes awry. The train lurches back and forth several times and the carpet onto which Adenoid Hynkel's guest of state, Benzino Napoloni is to alight from the train, is bundled in panic this way and that. Osterlich has still not been absorbed into the German Reich. When the real Mussolini hears about the annexation of Austria, he flies into a rage and grasps that Hitler is a glutton who will swallow down Italy when it suits him. This historical moment under the magnifying glass of comedy: the lackies chase about like insects. Everything takes place jumpily as in a bad dream, but not like in the newsreels accompanied by the dramatic voiceovers of Harry Giese. The horribly real is made clear in the distortion of the surreal grotesque: two flies in fantasy uniforms and their crazy, excited hum—forever trapped inside the double-glazed window of history.

Ignazio Silone also speaks of a carnival comedy in his early study *Der Fascismus* (Fascism) published in 1934 in neutral Switzerland, in which he says about Mussolini: 'He is doomed to play the Carnival Caesar for the rest of his life, to always have his facial muscles tensed so that the world can see the protruding Roman chin and the Napoleonic gaze. This obscene mixture of the present and the past makes contemporary Italian cultural life seem like a film.' And, Siegfried Kracauer, the cultural sociologist, who retrospectively documented the film industry of the Weimar Republic adds: 'Another feature of this world is that it extends deep into regions of the absurd; after all, absurdity becomes a necessity when the unfulfilled must be regarded as fulfilled. As a result of its consistent and at the same time absurd character, pseudo-reality has something of the drawing of a madman come to life.'

But humour, Jewish or not, never lets go when it comes to exposing totalitarian hubris. In Paris, the surrealists poured enthu-siastically over press images like this. In their journal *Documents*, they presented evidence for the mass psychology of modernity. Photo documents, taken out of context, were supposed to get to the bottom of the spectacle. The human toe as a giant sculpture, dark genitals in close-up, the severed legs of cattle, a fetish mask, com-bined with the insignia of papal power like any other power—every-thing presented itself to them in the mirror of aesthetic alienation.

Even the words of the unknown SA-man, a right-thinking pedant, fit into this world of bloody Punch and Judy. He is the joke character in a surreal Grand Guignol, but he does not know it because he's German. Completely absorbed in the role of the uniformed subaltern, he becomes the accountant of incomprehensible events that he logs in every detail.

I regard this find (Photo-Hoffmann, Munich, Theresienstrasse) like a splinter in my own flesh. My ancestors, all little people— what kind of people they were can only be a matter of conjecture from the perspective of today. My predecessors—in a word that always seemed repulsive to me, my 'forefathers'—have now all disappeared in the darkness of past times, sunk along with the stage on which they played their roles, the small as well as the great ones, and delivered wholesale to the merciless laughter of posterity.

Zygmunt Baumann, *Retrotopia* (Cambridge: Polity, 2017).

Umberto Eco, 'Ur-Fascism', *The New York Review of Books*, 22 June 1995. Available at: https://bit.ly/3viZjof (last accessed on 11 June 2021).

Lutz Hachmeister, *Der Gegnerforscher. Die Karriere des SS-Führers Franz Alfred Six* (Munich: Beck, 1998).

Historians speak of polycracy in the Nazi state—the competing system of different departments that appeared overnight. Later, depending on the general political climate and the whims of the dictator, they were adapted to the real course of the war. For diplomats, academics, journalists, born bureaucrats of all kinds, this may have been a nightmare, but in the end they all set about competing to immediately fulfil the *Führer*'s requirements. They were trained to 'work towards the *Führer*', a formula found by Ian Kershaw, the British biographer of Hitler, in the files of a Prussian Secretary of State.

This was also what Franz Six and his colleagues from the relevant fields set about doing. In one of the units under his command, the plans for a coordinated Jewish policy were developed, in close consultation with the Gestapo. One of the most prominent of his protégés was Adolf Eichmann, whom Six immediately sent to Vienna after the accession of Austria in 1938, where he developed the model of a department dedicated to the expulsion and economic plundering of the Jews: the Central Office for Jewish Emigration. At that time, various ideas were still in circulation about the resettlement of the Jews: for example, an agreement with Zionist associations, which imagined a separate Jewish state in Palestine, under British mandate at the time; this led to the adventurous 'Madagascar Plan', which soon proved unworkable. Adolf Eichmann, later an expert in deportation, and SS-Sturmbannführer, Herbert Hagen, head of the department 'II/112: Jews' in the Security Department's main office, were sent on a business trip to Palestine, on the orders of Alfred Six, to explore the possibilities of an orderly deportation. However, the British authorities only allowed them to stay in Haifa for a day (26 September 1937), then they were expelled from the country and set about seeing what was possible in terms of negotiations on the Arab side from Cairo. The establishment of a German airline to Palestine was discussed with the Jewish negotiator Feivel Polkes, official of the secret military organization 'Haganah'.

As little came of this idea as the plans discussed a year later, at the International Conference on Refugees in Evian, to distribute the Jews as asylum seekers on a quota basis to the participating countries. For now, the borders were closed. The ship was full, as the expression goes, a phrase which appears on cue with every wave of refugees. After Hitler unleashed the war, the course was set for the extermination of European Jews. From then on, they were treated as potential opponents, the trains travelled to Chelmo, Belzec, Sobibor, Treblinka and Auschwitz. Six million (and more) Jewish people were fed into the killing machine by the those driving the policy of extermination. The courts later had only to clarify who was directly or indirectly involved in it. Someone like Alfred Six stands for the elite of those planners, those who escaped undetected—he represents the cool functionary of the hour. According to Adorno, this coldness was 'the basic principle of bourgeois subjectivity, without which Auschwitz would not have been possible'. Or, in the treacherous language of the murderers: 'You don't fight rats with a revolver, but with poison and gas . . .' (Memorandum of the Munich SD Headquarters to Reinhard Heydrich).

Paul Celan, *Der Meridian, Endfassung—Vorstufen—Materialien*, Tübinger Ausgabe (Frankfurt am Main: Suhrkamp, 1999); *The Meridian: Final Version—Drafts—Materials* (Bernhard Böschenstein and Heino Schmull eds, Pierre Joris trans.) (Stanford, CA: Stanford University Press, 2003).

Karl Philipp Moritz, *Anton Reiser. Ein psychologischer Roman* (Berlin, 1785–90); *Anton Reiser: A Psychological Novel* (Ritchie Robertson trans.) (London: Penguin Classics, 2001).

Wilhelm Hausenstein, *Licht unter dem Horizont. Tagebücher von 1942 bis 1946* (Munich: F. Bruckmann Verlag, 1967).

'The events and things happening around the *Führer* are all *as if made for film*: nothing happens by itself, for its own sake, [. . .] everything becomes "current" only in *reproduction*, as a *cinematic* process. [. . .] *It is important to understand that everything between*

155

1933 and 1945 that seemed indifferent in immediate reality, so to speak, became in contrast effective in reproduction. This *shift* in relations explains much of what would otherwise be incomprehensible: one transforms realities into cinema in order to evade responsibility for reality and, to enjoy in the common form of reproduction called cinema, the special accent that is otherwise the prerogative of pornographic photography' (6 May 1945). The publicist and art historian Wilhelm Hausenstein wrote these astonishing sentences in his diary on 6 May 1945, shortly before the end of the war. Three days later, he soberly states: 'It is frightening, no horrifying, to see that the catastrophe does not bring about any moral change in human beings.' 'Thus the ordinary German supporter of Hitler allowed every stream to pass through him: the Jewish laws, the bombardment of the cities, the garrotting of officers, every disgrace, even the most unspeakable; he allowed them to pass through him as if through an *immune* organism.'

George Weidenfeld, with Derek Sington, *The Goebbels Experiment: A Study of the Nazi Propaganda Machine* (London: Murray, 1942).

One of the first serious studies of 'political marketing', using the example of the Reich Propaganda Ministry and his diabolical *spiritus rector* Joseph Goebbels. The author, the offspring of a Jewish family in Vienna, was nineteen years old when Hitler announced the accession of Austria in his Heldenplatz speech. Weidenfeld emigrated to London and worked for the BBC and, given his knowledge of the German situation, mainly for the Overseas Service. It was in this period at the beginning of the Second World War that his analysis of the Nazi propaganda techniques came into being and grew into a study on the role of the mass media and advertising strategies in modern societies. Weidenfeld worked as a journalist after the war and as a publisher (among others of Vladimir Nabokov's scandalous novel *Lolita*) and was one of the most sought-after experts in political media theory. He advised various heads of state and published their memoirs (de Gaulle, Adenauer, Golda Meir, Kissinger, Shimon Peres). In 1969, the Queen bestowed a peerage on him for services to England.

Lord Weidenfeld is the founder of the series of lectures named after him at St Anne's College, Oxford University. The present lectures were delivered in that series in May 2019.

Gilles Deleuze, *Essays Critical and Clinical* (Daniel W. Smith and Daniel W. Greco trans) (Minneapolis: University of Minnesota Press, 1997).

Walter Benjamin, *Über den Begriff der Geschichte* (Frankfurt am Main: Suhrkamp, 1950); 'Theses on the of Philosophy of History' in *Illuminations: Essays and Reflections* (Hannah Arendt ed., Harry Zohn trans.) (Boston: Mariner Books, 2019).

Ingeborg Bachmann, Quotation without source.

A NOTE ON THE TEXT

These essays are reworked and expanded versions of a series of four lectures presented by Durs Grünbein at St Anne's College, Oxford as the Weidenfeld Professor of Comparative European Literature in the summer of 2019.

ACKNOWLEDGEMENTS

Above all I owe a debt of gratitude to Karen Leeder, Professor at New College, Oxford, without whom these lectures would never have come into being. She was on hand throughout with advice and support and supplied me with the English version on schedule and ready for each lecture.

Durs Grünbein

A NOTE ON THE IMAGES

The images on the following pages have been reproduced from the post-card archive of Durs Grünbein, courtesy the author: 5, 17 (photograph by Heinrich Hoffmann), 24, 27, 33, 38, 41, 44, 52, 53 (photograph by Dörte Schmidt/Transocean), 57, 62 (detail from the painting *Ascent to Irschenberg* by Wolf Panizza), 63, 65, 74 (press photo, Dresden), 86, 87, 90, 91 (photograph by Walter Hahn), 95, 97, 99, 108, 118, 150 (photograph by Heinrich Hoffmann).

PAGES 9, 11, 13. Images courtesy Edmund Kalb Archiv / Rudolf Sagmeister.

PAGE 17. Photograph by Heinrich Hoffmann; courtesy Bayerische Staats-bibliothek München / Bildarchiv.

PAGE 84. Image from page 75 of exhibition catalogue *Britain at War*, The Museum of Modern Art, New York (23 May 23–2 September 1941). Digital image © 1941, The Museum of Modern Art, New York / Scala, Florence.

PAGE 89. Photograph courtesy Dresdner Hefte: *Beiträge zur Kultur-geschichte*, published by Dresdner Geschichtsverein (Issue 1, 1998).

PAGE 91. Image courtesy SLUB Dresden / Deutsche Fotothek / Walter Hahn.

PAGE 123. This photograph of Franz Six is available in the public domain.

PAGE 144. 'The Ghetto in Luck', newspaper article pasted with comments in the margin; Anna Haag's Diary, 12 December 1942; image courtesy Sabine Brügel-Fritzen (Anna-Haag-Estate).

PAGE 150. Photograph by Heinrich Hoffmann; courtesy the National Archives at College Park, Maryland, USA.